THE TRUE VINE AND ME

A Seven-Week Bible Study

TONI SHILOH

Cover design by Toni Shiloh.

Cover art photos © DepositPhotos.com/kishivan used by permission.

Malibu script font © Creativefabrica.com used by permission.

Edited by Katie Donovan.

Published in the United States of America by Toni Shiloh.

www.ToniShiloh.com

Created with Vellum

DEDICATION

To the Author and Finisher of my faith.

INTRODUCTION

I have been a lover of stories for as long as I can remember. My mind has the ability to plop me right into the setting at the prompting of the author. When I began reading my Bible as an adult, that love of story magnified tenfold. The Author gave me an intense desire to want to understand every word and seek a deeper knowledge in the life-giving stories that are shared in the sixty-six books that comprise the Bible.

Jesus as the True Vine is an image that has always brought me immense peace. Yet it wasn't until I taught a lesson on the very subject to the wonderful women of Holy Trinity Church in McLean, Virginia, that I truly understood how much God is in the details.

It's my deepest desire to take you to the vineyard so you may experience the True Vine and the abiding love of the Vinedresser. I know the Father and Son have much to teach us. I know that no matter how many times I reread this study or participate in discussions that form from it, God will continue to teach me something new, and that is my prayer for you as well.

Come alongside me as we rest in the vineyard with the True Vine and the Vinedresser and learn the secrets They have to share.

How to Use This Study

The True Vine and Me is meant to be used by individuals or small groups. Please, take your time and work at your own pace for any daily materials. There are two days of rest built into each week so you can catch up as time permits or merely reflect on the week's lesson.

A Prayer for You

Heavenly Father,

Thank You for each and every person who opens this book. May You meet him/her between these pages as they dive into who You are as the Vinedresser and who Jesus is as the True Vine. Please bring the Word alive for them and nourish their spirit through the True Vine. For those coming together as a group, please encourage them to be open and vulnerable. May Your presence rest over that body like a warm hug, and may the Spirit be alive in their conversations. As we commit to sharing the messy that is life and the joy You bring, may we continue to grow and be more fruitful. Not just as the body but as the individual fruit You made us to be.

In Jesus's Name,

Amen.

THE VINEDRESSER

I am the true vine, and My Father is the vinedresser.

—JOHN 15:1

A FRUIT IS ONLY AS GOOD AS THE SOURCE OF ITS NOURISHMENT FOR growth and the caretaker overseeing its fruitfulness. The Vinedresser has the heavy task of maintaining the vines in the vineyard and making sure they're pruned accurately to yield maximum fruit.

Vinedresser - a person who cultivates and prunes grapevines*

Our Father, the ultimate Vinedresser, must assess the soil the vine will be planted in. He needs to know the perfect location for the vineyard to flourish and what climate will be perfect for the vines to weather under.

* *Merriam-Webster.com Dictionary*, entry for "vinedresser," accessed July 24, 2024, https://www.merriam-webster.com/dictionary/vinedresser.

Then there's the actual planting of the vineyard. Consideration must be made for orienting the rows—the space between each vine—and how to amend the soil if the current one is unsatisfactory. God is the master Vinedresser and knows exactly what type of climate we need to thrive.

The good Lord sent us Jesus Christ, the True Vine, so that we would forever be connected to our Father through repentance of sin and reconciliation. Understanding the power of the True Vine and what that means for us will only enrich our faith journey as we navigate the ups and downs the world throws at us.

As we walk through this seven-week study, take time to reflect on God's goodness in how He cares for you, the branch. Ask God to reveal to you the ways He has used your location to shape and mature you. Seek Him daily to discover the ways He's called you, set you apart, matured you, and uniquely crafted you. He wants a deeper relationship with you and is more than happy to talk with you.

When we take time to explore the beauty of the vineyard and understand just how much the Vinedresser does for us, our perspective shifts from inward to outward. Our eyes lift from self and the problems before us to above, the Creator of the universe.

> My help comes from the Lord,
>   Who made heaven and earth.
>
> — PSALM 121:2

Without the care of the Vinedresser, we would perish. We would be like a potted plant that has been neglected and withered away. It droops and is lifeless. Thank God we are connected to a source that is everlasting.

> Have you not known?
> Have you not heard?
> The everlasting God, the Lord,
> The Creator of the ends of the earth,
> Neither faints nor is weary.
> His understanding is unsearchable.
>
> — ISAIAH 40:28

From the beginning He had a plan to keep us connected to Him. To ensure we walked in relationship on a daily basis. Before the sin of Adam and Eve, that plan was here on earth. Now, in the in-between of waiting for Jesus's return, that plan exists on the spiritual realm. Thanks to the gift of the Holy Spirit, we can flourish in this life and for promised eternity.

This study will help us see that God's plan is always for our benefit and good. Not just as individuals but as the body of Christ at large. Let's take this appointed time to foster our relationship with the Holy Trinity and learn more about God's will for our lives.

A Prayer

Heavenly Father,

We invite You into this place, into our hearts. As we commit ourselves to this study, may we come to realize just how majestic You are as the Vinedresser. Take us through the vineyard and show us Your heart for Your people. Open our ears to hear and our eyes to see what knowledge You wish to impart to us. Give us hearts that are understanding and spirits that are willing to experience You in a new way. May our hearts be changed forever and our relationships with You grow and bear fruit in our lives that overflows to others.

In Jesus's name,

Amen.

WEEK 1

Location, Location, Location

DAY 1

The Move

The vinedresser has the most important job. A vineyard will not exist without the love and care he gives to deciding the particulars. A vineyard does not exist without his desire to first create one. In order for a vineyard to thrive, the vinedresser knows choosing the location is one of the most important decisions he must make.

In oenology (the science of wine and winemaking), location is a factor that falls under *aspect*. "The aspect of a vineyard is the direction that a slope faces, which is an important feature of vineyard locations."*

This week we'll explore location...*your* location.

If you've ever wondered why God has you in a certain place, then this lesson is for you. If you love where you live, then this week is still for you. You are not on that street by whim, but a greater design is at work.

Let's get started. **Read Genesis 12.**

* "What is called the aspect of a vineyard?," Oray-Wine, posted August 19, 2023, https://oray-wine.com/en/what-is-called-the-aspect-of-a-vineyard/.

Now the Lord had said to Abram:
"Get out of your country,
From your family
And from your father's house,
To a land that I will show you."

— GENESIS 12:1

The Vinedresser knows exactly what kind of environment is best for you. He knows how the makeup of your family, childhood experiences, and trials have and will shape you.

When we look at the Israelites as our examples, we see a man (Abram) who was called out of his current location—Ur (Genesis 11) —to a promised land.

God knew Abram would be a blessing to all peoples on earth (Genesis 12:3), but first, the Vinedresser needed Abram to be set apart first. Abram needed to be moved.

What is it about a move that stresses you out?

____

____

____

____

Abram was seventy-five when he was called. He moved from Ur to Haran with his wife, nephew, servants, and all his possessions (Genesis 12:4-5).

Though Abram was obedient to the call, we see him wrestle with his humanity (and all the corresponding doubts that follow) in subsequent chapters in Genesis. We see him lie about Sarai being his wife. We see him doubt the promise of an heir by conceiving a child with Hagar (his wife's slave), when it was Sarai the one true heir was to come through.

We don't see the conviction he must have felt after committing some of these actions. However, we are privy to his growth when God asks him to sacrifice Isaac, his true heir, on an altar. Abraham (name change comes in Genesis 17) immediately obeys, and God sees that Abraham has grown and borne fruit of faithfulness.

Sometimes we read these biblical accounts and feel ashamed for our own doubts. Did we really hear God ask us to move from point A to E? If we're supposed to live in this new town, then why are all these bad things happening?

Would your faith grow if you never experienced hardships?

____

____

____

____

Sometimes we see trials as punishment from God, but that is not always the case. Sometimes difficulties come as a result of our own bad decisions because we failed to check in with the Lord first. Hardships can also come from living in a broken world, a direct result of the sin committed in the Garden of Eden.

Our bodies are broken because of the sin prevalent in the world. We suffer from illnesses like cancer and autoimmune disorders which cause physical and mental hardships. Death, watching a loved one suffer, mental health disorders all contribute to the overwhelming suffering in the world.

In these moments, prayer and quiet time with the True Vine is essential. We need to ensure we're connected to Jesus so we can endure whatever obstacles come our way. We also need to nourish our spiritual self. And just like the man in Mark 9:24, we can always ask the Lord to help our unbelief. In fact, that's part of the growth process we experience in the vineyard, but we'll discuss that later.

Back to Abraham.

Each time Abraham moved, he accrued wealth in livestock and possessions. It became so much that he had to split off from his nephew in order to have room for it all.

Unfortunately, not all moves are because our possessions have increased exponentially. Sometimes a move can bring a stripping away of possessions. Maybe it's because you're intentionally downsizing, you lost all your possessions, or material wealth may have become an idol to you. Maybe the Lord knows all our stuff will only weigh us down in our new journey.

Are you in a season of material gain or stripping away? How has God's hand been in your season?

____

____

____

____

Whenever you move, instead of listing the ways it'll inconvenience you—and it will, without a doubt—make a list of things God is doing through your new location. Your list might have these possible blessings: near to family, a good school district for your children, a promotion and better income for the family, an opportunity to meet new people to share the Gospel with, etc.

Believe me, there's a reason God is allowing the move to happen. If you cannot find any earthly benefits for the move, think spiritually. Which aspect of the fruit of the Spirit (Galatians 5:22-24) could be growing because of your physical location? Remember, nothing is wasted with God.

> And we know that all things work together for good to those who love God, to those who are the called according to His purpose.
>
> — ROMANS 8:28

A Prayer

Heavenly Father,

Thank You for knowing exactly what I need at my current location, whether it's less or more. Thank You for setting me apart for something greater to come. Please give me ears to hear what You want me to learn at this time. Please give me eyes to see the joy that can be experienced at this new location. Please give me a heart to understand Your plan for my life and a spirit that's willing to go where You call me to go. I pray that I will not veer off the path You have set me on.

In Jesus's Name,

Amen.

DAY 2

The Call

So he said to Him, "O my Lord, how can I save Israel?"

— JUDGES 6:15A

Have you ever had a moment with God where you knew specifically He was calling you to do something for Him? Maybe that task was small, a one-time event, or maybe it was the larger calling on your life that led to your purpose in the kingdom.

Did doubts immediately follow?

In Judges 6, we're introduced to Gideon. He was from the "weakest" clan in Manasseh and considered himself to be the "least in [his] family" (Judges 6:15). Gideon had doubts he could be of any use to the Lord.

But he's not the only person that ever doubted in the Bible.

Read Exodus 3.

But Moses said to God, "Who am I that I should go to Pharaoh, and that I should bring the children of Israel out of Egypt?"

— EXODUS 3:11

God is not surprised when He chooses a person to participate in His plan for humanity. He knows your deepest secrets, your desires, and exactly how you will respond when He asks you to step out in faith.

The person who is surprised is you.

You don't know what you're made of until you're walking the path God sets you on. Answering the call requires an unwavering trust in God. It is only our fear that keeps us from saying "Here I am" immediately and unwaveringly.

Have you ever asked the Lord, "Who am I?"

____

____

____

____

The Bible is full of people who have answered the call of the Lord but had doubts when God shared His plan.

Moses believed his speech disqualified him. Gideon thought his status in his family made him unworthy. Even Saul (1 Samuel 9) had the same feeling of inadequacy that Gideon suffered from. Esther thought she did not have enough influence in her sphere.

None of that mattered because "with God all things are possible" (Matthew 19:26b).

Do you think if you were able to answer God's call immediately, without hesitation, because you *believed* yourself to be equipped, your obedience would have the same impact and weight as when answered from a position of ill-preparedness?

God knows where you feel lacking. God turned Moses from someone afraid to speak into someone who became a prophet and a judge of His people. God took Gideon from self-doubt to leading three hundred mighty men against the Midianites. Saul became a great king, God's anointed one, who led many battles. After reading the book of Esther, we learn Esther becomes a queen created "for such a time as this" (Esther 4:14).

List a few fears you believe keep you from being used by God.

____

____

____

____

Are you ready to surrender your fears? Are you ready for God to show you exactly how He created you to be? Answering His call is one of the ways you become more fruitful. The growing process stretches us, but it's necessary. We must be pruned of those insecurities that hold us in bondage and keep us from being readily obedient. We need to make way for the righteous fruit to bloom under God's care and guidance.

Because every single time you feel inferior, unworthy, or (insert your fear), you are given an opportunity to lean on God and not your own strength. Let God show you just how strong He can be. Empty yourself of fear, of inadequacies, of lack of self-worth.

Friend, I know it's easier said than done. I've had many times where I did not trust in my abilities to get something done. But the wonderful thing about being called by God is He never asks you to do the task alone.

> And lo, I am with you always, even to the end of the age.
>
> — MATTHEW 28:20B

You were created exactly the way God needed you to be. You are your own grape. There is no other like you, and there will never be one like you when you cease to exist on earth. You are a one-of-a-kind because that is how the Lord operates. He creates one person for a certain purpose. Noah could not have done Moses's job and vice versa.

Spend time in silence with the Lord. Ask Him to reveal the current call on your life. Remember that calls can change. You may be in a season that leaves you more available for certain tasks. Or you may be in a season where the immediate members of your household are all you need to be concerned about. You won't know until you ask the Lord and wait patiently for His answer.

What is God calling you into?

____

____

____

____

____

A Prayer

Heavenly Father,

Thank You for the call You've placed on my life. I ask that You give me ears to hear You every step of the way in this journey. Please give me eyes to see the details of this call that I need to continue to grow in. Please give me a heart that is understanding of who You are, who I am in You, and who You want me to be in this phase of life. Please bless me with a spirit that is willing to be obedient despite my fears. Please prune me of my insecurities so that I will readily say "Yes, Lord" to Your next call. May I glorify You in all that I do.

In Jesus's name,

Amen.

DAY 3

Set Apart

Set apart - to keep or intend for a special purpose*

ON DAY ONE, I SPOKE OF HOW GOD MOVED ABRAM IN ORDER TO set him apart from others. There are many lessons we can learn by reading the Old Testament and tracking the movements of the Israelites. We see Abram start out on a pilgrimage to the Promised Land. We see the Israelites become enslaved by the Egyptians—where they still were set apart from the Egyptians—and then be delivered by Moses and begin another journey toward the Promised Land. The Lord explained to His chosen people how they had to rid the Promised Land of the current occupants so that they would not defile themselves or defile the land (Leviticus 17:24-30).

You see, God is holy. As His people—those who have accepted the Lord Jesus as their savior and repented of their sins—we are called to live holy lives. We are to be set apart from sin so that we can be used by God for His purpose.

---

* *Merriam-Webster.com Thesaurus*, entry for "set apart," accessed April 2, 2024, https://www.merriam-webster.com/thesaurus/set%20apart.

Being set apart does not mean we never make another mistake. The Israelites' journey in the wilderness shows this to be true. What being set apart does is start a process where we posture ourselves in front of the Lord in a way that says *I'm listening, Lord.*

It's like prayer.

> And when you pray, you shall not be like the hypocrites. For they love to pray standing in the synagogues and on the corners of the streets, that they may be seen by men. Assuredly, I say to you, they have their reward. But you, when you pray, go into your room, and when you have shut your door, pray to your Father who is in the secret place; and your Father who sees in secret will reward you openly.
>
> — MATTHEW 6:5-6

Prayer time is another period where we specifically set ourselves apart to petition or intercede before God. We prioritize these moments into our schedules. We may have a special place in our homes where we pray (not that we can't pray anywhere). We even have the Lord's Prayer to show us how to pray (Matthew 6:9-13).

Is it any wonder that God will set us apart physically, mentally, and spiritually as well?

How is the Lord setting you apart in your current season of life?

> For whom He foreknew, He also predestined to be conformed to the image of His Son, that He might be the firstborn among many brethren.
>
> — ROMANS 8:29

When God sets us apart, He puts us on a path to become more like His Son, Jesus. This helps us grow in righteousness and is known as the sanctification process. It's also a mark of fruitfulness. We are meant to bear more fruit because we are connected to the True Vine.

Yet so many times, we fail to look at our favor in good terms. When we're in the workforce and can't seem to find a friendly face, we feel isolated. Sometimes we may even choose to behave like others because we don't want to be different. But perhaps the reason you are in that job, in that office, is to shine a light in darkness. You are an instrument of God's holiness, and conforming to the world's pattern goes against His intention for our lives. Thank goodness He can redeem anything.

Maybe you're still in a school environment and don't get along with all the trends that are currently popular. You fear there's something wrong with you, but I'm here to tell you there's not. You've been set apart. God's call is on your life, and He is already taking steps to separate you from something that could impede your progress. **Read Gideon 7.**

How did God set apart the three hundred? For what purpose?

___

___

___

Remember, your current location does not always resemble the Promised Land. At times, it resembles a vast desert with an abundance of tumbleweeds. But have no fear. You will not dry out. You will not wither away as long as you stay connected to the True Vine.

God set you apart for a purpose. Trust Him to reveal it in a way unique to you and in His perfect timing.

> Call to Me, and I will answer you, and show you great and mighty things, which you do not know.
>
> —JEREMIAH 33:3

Take the time to allow God to change your perspective. See your difference as the mark of God on your life. See being separated from others as God growing the specific fruit you need for a future task. Begin to search for His handiwork and footprints, the evidence that He's walking alongside you in the desert.

A Prayer

Heavenly Father,

Thank You for setting me apart. For all the times I've felt isolated in a world of darkness, thank You for isolating me from sin. Please give me understanding of what You are doing. Regardless of what I may go through, I pray I will call to You and seek You first and foremost. Please share with me the things I do not know so I may continue to be strengthened by the True Vine as You set me apart for Your good works.

In Jesus's name,

Amen.

DAY 4

The Soil

The worse the soil, the better the wine.

— UNKNOWN

FERTILE SOIL IS SOMETHING WE OFTEN PRAY FOR WHEN IT COMES to God planting scripture into our hearts. After reading the Parable of the Sower (Matthew 13), Christians don't want to be the type of believer that doesn't receive God's word on fertile ground. However, when it comes to winemaking, fertile soil will not produce the best wines.

Have you ever seen a celebrity rise to the top, and when they sit down to be interviewed, you discover just how harrowing their journey has been up to that point? Their life is never easy. Well, similarly, the trials and tribulations you go through contribute to your soil, metaphorically speaking.

> "Chalk soils tend to be low in fertility as well, which is another benefit as it's easier to add nutrients than reduce them."*

* Caroline Gilby, "Winemaking: The Importance of the Soil," *The Wine Society*, June

The reason winemaking doesn't require fertile soil is because the vinedresser will add the necessary nutrients to fit the wine being created. Just like the earthly example, the Lord must add the spiritual nutrients *you* need to create the perfect soil for growth.

The rocky soil that exists on the surface of the vineyard could be compared to building a "house on the rock."

> Therefore whoever hears these sayings of Mine, and does them, I will liken him to a wise man who built his house on the rock
>
> — MATTHEW 7:24

Think back to your past. What trials have you gone through that produced spiritual fruit in your life? Can you now be thankful for them and rejoice in God's work in your life?

____

____

____

____

My youngest son has sickle cell anemia. It's a disease that can cause intense pain, blood getting stuck in organs, etc. He has already had three surgeries and countless hospital stays. But I am now at the place where the first thing I do is pray for my son's health and healing the minute it looks like a sickle cell complication could arise. I don't fret as much as I used to because I have years of experience proving

---

22, 2020. https://www.thewinesociety.com/discover/explore/expertise/winemaking-the-importance-of-the-soil.

God answers prayers. God sees my son, hears him, and loves him more than I do. This same God has blessed my son with surgeries that were complication free. Even the ones that weren't, still God worked in them. It got to the point in the worst of my son's trials that I closed my eyes and whispered, *"Bless the Lord, O my soul; and all that is within me, bless His holy name!"* (Psalm 103:1).

I would not have the fruit of *faithfulness* if God had not been present in those health trials. He didn't create these difficult situations, but He surely provided the nutrients I needed in order to learn how to lean on Him.

> My brethren, count it all joy when you fall into various trials, knowing that the testing of your faith produces patience.
>
> —JAMES 1:2-3

How can you look at your trials as a blessing and a tool to grow you spiritually?

___

___

___

___

In the Old Testament, the Israelites put stones of remembrance together to remember what God had done. **Read Joshua 4**.

Can you look at the stones in your past and see the handiwork of God? Often times we want to shy away from hardship or ignore it completely, but God does not let anything go to waste. He's building a solid foundation for you to live by, and the Rock of Ages will see you through.

A Prayer

Heavenly Father,

Thank You for the trials You have brought me through. Thank You for the lessons You taught me and the fruit You've grown through these situations. It's hard to not want to wish the trial away or make it go by quicker. Please help me to count it pure joy because You are at work. May I never forget that there will be the other side of the trial, and I will have the blessing of looking back and seeing the growth of my faith.

In Jesus's Name,

Amen.

DAY 5

Unique

I took my uniqueness and treated it like a horn.

— BILLY PAUL

In a world where we're constantly hearing the uniqueness of everyone, being special feels underwhelming. How can I feel unique when *everyone* is unique?

But you are unique because God only made one of you. It's as simple, and as complicated, as that. Even if you're an identical twin, you still have your own personality and your own gifts. You *are* unique.

Then again, maybe that's the scary part. Being unique comes with pressure. How am I different, and is that difference a good thing? Am I supposed to do something special in life because there's only one of me? What if I fail the Lord because I failed to recognize my unique calling?

Honestly, I could probably go on and on about the many ways that being unique can strike fear. Instead, I want you to take a moment to think about the ways you are different and why that might make you apprehensive.

Why do you fear being unique?

____

____

____

____

The enemy does *not* want us to embrace our uniqueness and the call God has on our life specifically. If he can spin us up to where we're paralyzed in fear, all the better. If he can kill our desire to walk by faith by using death by comparison, then he will do so.

How does this relate to the vineyard? Why am I harping on our uniqueness?

Glad you asked. Did you know that every wine has a specific terroir they need to grow in?

> Terroir - the environment the grapevine grows in, including climate, terrain and cultivation methods...in addition to the soil itself.*

However, not every grape can grow in the same terroir. That's why you have different types of grapes grown in one region versus another. No one would confuse white wine with red wine, or if you're a wine connoisseur, a Pinot Grigio with a Pinot Noir.

Why then do we compare ourselves to another? Whether it's simply comparing how one woman dresses to the clothes in your clos-et., or how another person's talent seems to be leaps and bounds

* "Talking Terroir: The Dirt on Soil for Wine," King Estate Winery, posted November 29, 2016, https://kingestate.com/talking-terroir-the-dirt-on-soil/.

ahead of yours. When we compare, we take our focus off Jesus and spiral downward in the comparison trap.

You were not meant to bloom where another was planted.

Do you remember the Parable of the Sower? To refresh your memory, please **read Matthew 13:1-9, 18-23**.

> But he who received seed on the good ground is he who hears the word and understands it, who indeed bears fruit and produces: some a hundredfold, some sixty, some thirty.
>
> — MATTHEW 13:23

Each seed yielded different amounts of produce, *some a hundredfold, some sixty, some thirty.* If the same seed can yield different amounts, doesn't it stand to reason that people would be the same way? Having a different product yield does not mean you are unfruitful.

I'm a writer and I've written more than thirty books (as of this book's publication). I also have many writer friends, all with talent I admire. Yet each one of us has written a different number of books. If I pooled just the ones who have been writing the same length of time I have, we would still have varying amounts. That doesn't mean that I'm better than the ones who've written fewer books than I or that I'm less than the authors who have written more. It simply means we are operating in the way God created us to operate.

We have got to get off the comparison train and turn toward our Heavenly Father and ask Him what He wants.

> But seek first the kingdom of God and His righteousness, and all these things shall be added to you.
>
> — MATTHEW 6:33

List a few talents you possess that you believe are gifted from God. What would it look like to stop comparing and surrender to God's pacing?

Being unique is a tool created by God. He wants us to be able to lean on Him and seek Him first in everything. If we were all the same, the chances of us seeking our neighbor first instead of God would rise. Why would we seek Him if we could just ask them how to sing the best? But when our product looks different, we have to seek the Lord for understanding.

Being unique also brings about a closeness with the Lord. We have no choice but to recognize His penmanship in our lives.

> I will praise You, for I am fearfully *and* wonderfully made;
> Marvelous are Your works,
> And *that* my soul knows very well.
>
> — PSALM 139:14

A Prayer

Heavenly Father,

Thank You for the unique way in which You knit me. Thank You for the talents You've bestowed upon me. May I use them at Your pacing, for Your glory. Please show me the ways I am comparing myself to others and/or moving at a pace that is not my own. Whether You need to slow me down or speed me up, I surrender to Your perfect timing.

In Jesus's Name,

Amen.

WEEK 2

The True Vine

DAY 1

The Scion

Scion - 2: a detached living portion of a plant (such as a bud or shoot) joined to a stock in grafting and usually supplying solely aerial parts to a graft.*

I love a word that has more than one meaning, especially when a word can represent the earthly view as well as a spiritual view. The word *scion* is such a word.

I'm not going to lie, my first introduction to the word was the car made by Toyota. In fact, my husband and I have owned multiple Scion xBs, and we loved each of those cars. However, as I was conducting research, I came across this word in the vineyard sense.

You see, most vineyards begin by grafting a vine to a scion. It's vital that this scion be resistant to pests so that it can thrive in its planted location and not be plagued by them or diseases.

We have been connected to the True Vine, the Scion. He has proven Himself to be resistant to temptation. Not in a superior way that would condemn us for being weak and giving in, but with all

---

* *Merriam-Webster.com Thesaurus*, entry for "scion," accessed May 5, 2024, https://www.merriam-webster.com/thesaurus/scion.

humility and love, providing a merciful place to accept forgiveness or to heed His way of escape.

An earthly scion is a hybrid taking two different genetic vines and breeding a new creation that can withstand more than either one alone could. Sounds like our Savior, doesn't it?

Fully Man. Fully God.

He defeated the grave so that we could be reconciled to the Father. And all we have to do is be grafted to Him.

> Abide in Me, and I in you. As the branch cannot bear fruit of itself, unless it abides in the vine, neither can you, unless you abide in Me.
>
> —JOHN 15:4

Scion - 1a: descendant of a wealthy, aristocratic, or influential family*

Remember when I was talking about that other meaning of *scion*? Besides it being a strong vine, it's a descendant from an aristocratic family.

If you **read Matthew 1:1-17**, you'll see all the great people in Jesus's lineage. From notables like Abraham, Rahab, and Ruth, to David, Josiah, and Joseph, Jesus came from an influential family. He's known as the *Lion of Judah,* a nod to the Israelite tribe He hails from. I can't help but see God's handiwork in the definition of *scion.* God is always in the details.

* *Merriam-Webster.com Thesaurus*, entry for "scion."

Do you have people in your lineage who have overcome hardships? Who have a deep-rooted faith in Jesus? If not, can you imagine how your descendants will feel when they think back to you and your abiding faith in the Lord?

But I'm not done explaining the awesomeness that is the Scion. The scion needs to be resistant to the natural pests that exist in the vineyard.

> Pest - **2:** something resembling a pest in destructiveness
> **3:** one that pesters or annoys*

Now I'm not calling the enemy a mere pest, but I'm sure you can draw the same parallels I can.

Read Matthew 4:1-11.

Can you see how the Lord resisted the enemy's temptation? That same power dwells in you.

> But if the Spirit of Him who raised Jesus from the dead dwells in you, He who raised Christ from the dead will also give life to your mortal bodies through His Spirit who dwells in you.
>
> — ROMANS 8:11

* *Merriam-Webster.com Thesaurus,* entry for "pests," accessed May 5, 2024, https://www.merriam-webster.com/thesaurus/pests.

He is our example, He is our life force. He gives us the ability to flee from the enemy and escape temptation, but we cannot do it in our own might. It's about praying to Him in the secret places so that when we struggle in the public places, we know what to do.

A Prayer

Lord Jesus,

Thank You for being fully Man and fully God. Thank You for grafting us into the True Vine. We know that any fruit we bear is because of time spent with You. As we go through this week, help us to see the opportunities to be still with You. To just sit and soak in Your presence and get to know You on a deeper level than we have before. We give all praise to You today and always.

In Jesus's name,

Amen.

DAY 2

Grafted In

Behold what manner of love the Father has bestowed on us, that we should be called children of God!

— 1 JOHN 3:1A

If you're reading this and do not have Jewish heritage, then in the terms of the Old Testament, you are a Gentile. Gentiles have been offered salvation through the goodness and mercy of God. We've been adopted into the kingdom of heaven. Praise God!

Read Romans 11.

There is a lot written and a lot I can say. To help you understand the beauty of being grafted into the vineyard by Christ's ultimate sacrifice, I had you read the whole chapter. One thing Jesus says over and over in John is for us to abide in Him. As you can see from reading Romans, not abiding can result in being cut off.

But let us focus on the grafting, on being children of God, of having sonship by His grace.

> Just as He chose us in Him before the foundation of the world, that we should be holy and without blame before Him in love, having predestined us to adoption as sons by Jesus Christ to Himself, according to the good pleasure of His will.
>
> — EPHESIANS 1:4-5

What does it mean to you to be grafted in?

___

___

___

___

We don't need to boast that we've been grafted in. It is a gift of mercy and love from our Father, the Great Vinedresser. We should also be fully aware that we are the branches, and the power is not in the branches but in the vine, a.k.a. the root.

> But if you do boast, remember that you do not support the root, but the root supports you.
>
> — ROMANS 11:18B

Without Jesus's sacrifice, we would be rootless and without the benefits of being grafted in. So what are the benefits?

1. We are now children of God.
2. We are holy.

3. We have eternal life.

Three simple truths that have eternal value. As a child of God, we are now co-heirs with Christ.

> The Spirit Himself bears witness with our spirit that we are children of God, and if children, then heirs—heirs of God and joint heirs with Christ, if indeed we suffer with Him, that we may also be glorified together.
>
> — ROMANS 8:16-17

As heirs, we are entitled to inherit a place in the kingdom of God. After all, Jesus Himself told us that He goes to make a place for us (John 14:2), and we can receive that through the inheritance of being a child of God.

Next, we're are now holy because Jesus is holy (Romans 11:16). Scripture tells us all we have to do is ask for Jesus to forgive us and make us right with God.

> If we confess our sins, He is faithful and just to forgive us our sins and to cleanse us from all unrighteousness.
>
> — 1 JOHN 1:9

What a beautiful gift, to be cleansed from unrighteousness by simply repenting and asking for forgiveness. It seems so simple, yet the ramifications are life-changing! That is the glory of God and the beauty of Jesus's love for us. He wants us to be reconciled to the Father because He knows what peace that brings.

Last but absolutely not the least, we will be gifted with eternal life with the Lord.

Read 1 Corinthians 15:50-58.

How I long for that heavenly body and that moment of worshipping the Lord.

These gifts are the beauty of being grafted into the True Vine. We have much to look forward to.

A Prayer

Heavenly Father,

Thank You for allowing me to be grafted into the True Vine. It is a gift I can never repay nor earn, but I receive it willingly with gratitude. Lord God, I ask that You help me remember the beauty of being your child. You are my Father, and that relationship means everything. I pray that I remember that Your Son made me holy by His righteousness. And last, I pray that I keep the hope of eternity in my heart and let it guide my actions.

In Jesus's name,

Amen.

DAY 3

Vintage Power

The older the vine, the sweeter the wine.

—ANONYMOUS

We've all heard the adage of aging like fine wine. It's something I heard and laughed at in my youth but have come to appreciate as I continue to get older. And when I researched the ins and outs of a vineyard, I came to understand just how much truth rests behind that statement.

I learned a lot about vintage power.

Did you know some believe the older the vine, the more flavor found in the grape? Can you imagine your fruitfulness showing up in such a way? After all, one of the benefits of remaining in Christ is becoming more fruitful. Not merely the amount of fruit individually showing in your life, but the depth of flavor each fruit holds on its own.

Do people think you're joyful because you always greet a person with a smile? Or is it because it radiates from the inside out? That's the concentrated flavor the Lord is going for. Not for you to merely be going through the motions—believe me, we've all been there, myself included—but for the fruit to shine from the heart on outward.

According to *Last Bottle*, when a vine begins to age, "The clusters become sparse, producing less fruit, and the skin-to-pulp ratio increases. This results in berries with more concentrated flavor."*

The thought of losing clusters and becoming a spiritual tree with less fruit is disconcerting. But it brings to mind the saying "quality over quantity." It's not about the amount. It's never been that way with God. *He* is the multiplier. If we have any fruit on our spiritual tree, it's because He cultivated it. Your character is His concern.

> For the Lord does not see as man sees; for man looks at the outward appearance, but the Lord looks at the heart.
>
> — 1 SAMUEL 16:7B

Being connected to the True Vine gives us direct access to vintage power. Christ was there in the beginning and is as old as time. And we have a direct link to that vintage power. As our spiritual walk with Christ deepens, the concentrated flavor in our fruit will began to show.

What does it mean to you to have direct access to the vintage power of Christ?

---

* "The Older the Vine, the Better the Wine...Truth or Fiction?," Last Bottle, posted February 4, 2016, https://blog.lastbottlewines.com/education/old-vines-better-wine/.

Another interesting fact I discovered from *Last Bottle* is that "growers believe old vines have much deeper roots that can reach more mineral deposits and pull more terroir from the earth."*

Do you remember discussing terroir in week one, day five? Being connected to an old vine will feed you the nutrients you needed to grow. Not surface-level nutrients but the kind of mineral deposits that give great character and flavor.

> But when the fullness of the time had come, God sent forth His Son, born of a woman, born under the law, to redeem those who were under the law, that we might receive the adoption as sons.
>
> — GALATIANS 4:4-5

God is all about timing. Nothing is rushed, nothing is hurried. He knows when you will grow a particular fruit to completion. When that fruit must rest for a moment while another one is tended to. He knew when to send Jesus to save man, and I can't help but think that timing was also another point of aging that benefits those who call themselves Christians.

When we live out a life that abides in the True Vine, we can be carefree in certain aspects. After all, we are connected to the one who gives us life. He satisfies our spiritual hunger, quenches our spiritual thirst. He sustains us daily; we have only to abide. He's done the heavy lifting. We can rest in that.

* "The Older the Vine, the Better the Wine...Truth or Fiction?," Last Bottle.

A Prayer

Heavenly Father,

Thank You for sending us the One who was there at the beginning. The Lord Jesus is better than any fine wine and is full of concentrated flavor. But God, You didn't keep goodness for Yourself. You desired to share it with us, to commune with us. Thank You Jesus, for being the True Vine that gives us all the nutrients we could ever want or need spiritually as we abide in You. May we hold these truths close in our heart and imprint them where we'll never forget.

In Your mighty Son's name,

Amen.

DAY 4

God with Us

"Behold, the virgin shall be with child, and bear a Son, and they shall call His name Immanuel," which is translated, "God with us."

— MATTHEW 1:23

UNLIKE OTHER RELIGIONS WHERE GOD IS FAR FROM HIS PEOPLE, Christianity has the one true God who dwells **with us**. We are not alone. We are not without guidance. We don't have to be filled with doubt that God exists, because He chooses to dwell with us. How blessed we are!

Before Jesus returned to heaven, He promised His spirit to those who would believe (Luke 24:49). Belief in the Son (and repentance of sin) gives us direct access to the Father through the Spirit that dwells with us.

> But the hour is coming, and now is, when the true worshipers will worship the Father in spirit and truth; for the Father is seeking such to worship Him. God is Spirit, and those who worship Him must worship in spirit and truth.
>
> —JOHN 4:23-24

In order to worship God, we must do it through the spirit and in believing God's truth.

What do you believe about the Father, Son, and Holy Spirit?

____

____

____

____

When I was in high school, I would get anxious every time I took a test, especially in my math courses. Oh, how my stomach would churn and I would feel ill. But I would whisper "'I can do all things through Christ who strengthens me (Philippians 4:13), including taking this math test" to myself and pray that God would be with me during the test.

To me, the act was born of desperation. I struggled with math and just wanted to do well. I had a good GPA that I didn't want to decline because I couldn't understand pre-calculus. Looking back, I know exactly what I hoped to happen in those moments.

> But the Helper, the Holy Spirit, whom the Father will send in My name, He will teach you all things, and bring to your remembrance all things that I said to you.
>
> —JOHN 14:26

In high school, I didn't have scripture memorized. I didn't read my Bible like I should have and I definitely didn't understand the wholeness of the Trinity or understand them as individuals—Father, Son, and Holy Spirit—either. Yet the Spirit still helped me remember the verse in Philippians.

Now, I can't tell you how I did on each individual test, but I'll never forget taking my final exam and walking out of school elated because I'd earned one hundred percent.

I had a tutor, I studied so much that I didn't want to deal with math ever again. I'm not discounting either of those things, but I am saying I would've been worse off if I hadn't prayed and sought the help of the Lord.

That is why He didn't leave us alone. He *knew* we would need help. God fully understands our limitations before we even do. Being gifted with the Spirit showcases just how good the Vinedresser is to us.

> Every good gift and every perfect gift is from above, and comes down from the Father of lights, with whom there is no variation or shadow of turning.
>
> —JAMES 1:17

List some of the ways the Holy Spirit has helped you.

God is good and He loves you. He knows that loneliness is a real issue people battle with, how you can feel unimportant and unseen in a room full of people. But you're not alone. Not when the God of the universe desires a relationship with you. He sees you. He *knows* you. He calls you child.

> For God so loved the world that He gave His only begotten Son, that whoever believes in Him should not perish but have everlasting life.
>
> —JOHN 3:16

A Prayer

Lord God,

Thank You for loving me. Thank You for seeing me. Thank You for knowing my limitations and sending help to me. I'm in awe of You and Your goodness. Thank You for the gift of belief. May the Spirit help me fan the flames of faith and seek You all the days of my life. May I learn to access the Holy Spirit and continue to connect with You in Your fullness.

In Jesus's name,

Amen.

DAY 5

Rest

> And on the seventh day God ended His work which He had done, and He rested on the seventh day from all His work which He had done. Then God blessed the seventh day and sanctified it, because in it He rested from all His work which God had created and made.
>
> — GENESIS 2:2-3

REST ISN'T EASY FOR EVERYONE. IN A SOCIETY THAT PUSHES FOR productivity and success, resting may be mistaken for laziness. The last thing anyone wants to be accused of is not being useful. There's shame that comes with that and a guilt that you're just not doing enough.

But those are lies the enemy throws at us like fiery darts to keep us in bondage and run us into burnout. God created rest because He Himself rested from His work. After creation, He saw that it was good and rested. He blessed the day and sanctified it.

Read Exodus 20:8-11.

God informs the Israelites that rest is required. It's a commandment. It's not something we *should* do but something we *must* do. Not just because we want to avoid sin but because we desire to obey the

Lord in thanks and gratitude for all He's done. Keeping this commandment falls under the great commandment (Matthew 22:37).

In fact, in a vineyard, there is productivity for eight months and then the vines rest for four, going into a dormant state when winter season kicks in. *Four* months! Can you imagine being able to take that much time off to rest? Most of us wouldn't know what to do with ourselves.

Depending on what day of the year we start (and whether or not it's a leap year), we can have fifty-two or fifty-three days of Sabbath rest. How many of those days can you say you abstained from work?

We've become a society that has carpool moms, businesses that are open twenty-four seven, and people who need to earn income whether because they're chasing after money or because inflation has us living paycheck to paycheck.

Yet our Father does not want us to worry about food, water, or clothing. He knows exactly what we need and when we'll need it. And that does not negate the requirement for rest.

Read Matthew 6:25-34.

The Bible states in verse 25, "Therefore I say to you, do not worry about your life..." yet it's something we constantly do.

I should know—I recently had a meltdown when balancing the family budget. Unexpectedly, we had received a lot of medical bills, and the pressure of ensuring everything got paid and making sure I would still be able to meet our regular bills was too much. In tears, I poured my heart out to my husband over the pressure of maintaining the budget. He gently urged me to take to my prayer closet *and* to remember Matthew 6 and how we should not worry.

God is our provider. To skip rest and continue working shows a lack of trust. Not to mention the needless worry and heartache that occurs.

> Offer the sacrifices of righteousness,
> And put your trust in the Lord.
>
> — PSALM 4:5

When was the last time you worried about finances and were tempted to skip the Sabbath to work? What did you learn from that?

We can rest because God cares for us. We can rest because if God made it a commandment, then there is purpose behind rest. It is not a waste to recharge your batteries. Whether you fall on the very introverted side of the spectrum and *know* without a doubt that you need rest, or fall on the very extroverted side of the spectrum and have to be coaxed to rest, or fall anywhere between those two extremes, you need rest.

We all do.

> I will both lie down in peace, and sleep;
> For You alone, O Lord, make me dwell in safety.
>
> — PSALM 4:8

Make a list of ways you can rest with the Lord.

A Prayer

Heavenly Father,

I thank You for being a God who rests. Thank You for showing me the importance of rest when You sent Your Son, who withdrew to pray and rest in You. May I learn to incorporate a daily, weekly, monthly, etc., rest. Please guide me and show me what's best for myself. Inform me of how much rest I need so that I can be recharged when I most need it. Show me how to connect with You on days of rest and strengthen our relationship.

In Jesus's name,

Amen.

WEEK 3

The Branches

DAY 1

Branches

Branch - 1. a natural subdivision of a plant stem*

As you can tell by now, I love to use definitions and scripture to explore the ways the Lord talks to us. I'm a firm believer that creation speaks of the Lord if we are willing to listen, observe, and speak to the Spirit of our findings. That's honestly how this study came about. My love for God, the Word, and dictionaries.

When I read about Jesus calling the church "the branches," I immediately looked up the definition. The first one listed in Merriam-Webster Dictionary is at the top of this page. The branches are nothing but "a natural" part of the "plant stem." When we turn to the Bible, we get a fuller picture.

Romans 11:17 tells us that we Gentiles (non-Jews) were grafted into the vine. Now we're a natural part of the system through adoption.

Read Ephesians 1:4-6.

---

* *Merriam-Webster.com Dictionary*, entry for "branch," accessed May 10, 2024, https://www.merriam-webster.com/dictionary/branch.

What does it mean to you to be grafted in and now considered part of the body of Christ?

___

___

___

___

The Lord has an amazing design for the world and for each individual. We are now part of a larger story in the making. Though we know the ending victory, we get to walk the middle of the story with the Spirit as our guide.

> Branch - 2. something that extends from or enters into a main body or source*

Our life stems from the Source. Jesus is the True Vine, and without Him, we would wither and die.

> Abide in Me, and I in you. As the branch cannot bear fruit of itself, unless it abides in the vine, neither can you, unless you abide in Me.
>
> —JOHN 15:4

Jesus Himself, tells us that we *must* abide in Him. We cannot leave our main source, or life for us ends.

---

* *Merriam-Webster.com Dictionary*, entry for "branch."

> For the wages of sin is death, but the gift of God is eternal life in Christ Jesus our Lord.
>
> — ROMANS 6:23

Being attached to the main source is a very good thing and speaks to the goodness of God. We want to be connected to the source of life at all times, and abiding in Christ is the answer. We'll delve more into that in later weeks, but please make note of how vital it is.

But that's not all that being a branch benefits us.

> Branch - 3. a part of a complex body*

When we are grafted into the vine, we become part of the body of Christ, and what a glorious thing that is! The book of Romans tells us:

> So we, being many, are one body in Christ, and individually members of one another.
>
> — ROMANS 12:5

We are no longer alone in this faith journey. If you were born into a family of believers, you may never have experienced isolation in faith. However, if you did not grow up in a community of believers, finding one is so important. There is nothing better than being surrounded by like-minded people who will consistently and constantly point you to Christ. Finding a church home is something that takes time and needs the Holy Spirit's guidance. Make sure you listen to where God wants to plant you in the church community.

Besides helping combat loneliness, being surrounded by believers spurs our own growth. It's the whole iron-sharpens-iron benefit (Proverbs 27:17). When we take the time to do life with other believ-

---

* *Merriam-Webster.com Dictionary*, entry for "branch"

we learn more about God as a Father, the Holy Spirit as the Comforter, and how to serve one another. Our focus turns outward as we interact with those who are not like us. Growth happens when we do life among other believers. That is something we should not neglect.

What are some of the benefits of being a branch of the True Vine?

____

____

____

____

A Prayer

Heavenly Father,

I thank You that Your creation displays Your intricate design. You spoke the world into existence, breathed life into my being, and showed me in the beauty around me exactly who You are. I want to rejoice in Your creation, including that of the body of Christ. Help me to see how valuable the branches are, as individuals and a community at large. I pray that I glorify You corporately.

In Jesus's name,

Amen.

DAY 2

Pruning

> Prune - to cut off or cut back parts of for better shape or more fruitful growth*

THERE'S SOMETHING ABOUT THE WORD *PRUNING* THAT TENDS TO make Christians cringe and shrink away. Surely the thought of a foot-long pruning shear that can cut into branches with ease terrifies the most faithful of us.

But the pruning process is not meant to harm but to cultivate better growth.

> And every branch that bears fruit He prunes, that it may bear more fruit.
>
> —JOHN 15:2B

God is a master horticulturist and He knows exactly what we need to flourish and thrive where He's planted us. In our limited view,

* *Merriam-Webster.com Dictionary*, entry for "prune," accessed May 11, 2024, https://www.merriam-webster.com/dictionary/prune.

we may think that the abundance we have in our life is necessary to keep thriving. If you live in a good home, drive a luxury vehicle, and never wonder where your next meal comes from, the thought of any of your possessions being pruned may make you want to hold on to the materials even tighter. And if you're on the side of lack, you may wonder what else is left to give.

But being pruned is not necessarily about what we possess on earth but what is growing in our heart.

> Not what goes into the mouth defiles a man; but what comes out of the mouth, this defiles a man.
>
> — MATTHEW 15:11

If you picture your heart as a garden and the Lord the master Gardener, you can understand the loving care He takes in caring for each individual plant. He plants, He waters, He prunes, He oversees each step to ensure the garden will bloom in glory.

We need to adopt a heart posture that allows us to be more self-aware of the weeds in our garden. God is a gentle God. He will not attack the weeds with a weed whacker. Instead, He'll study each issue and determine what needs to be removed. He'll look at each flowering bud and decide what stays and what will be sheared off so the remainder will bloom more freely.

So let's talk about the pruning process that happens here on earth. Pruning takes place after harvest. Yes, I said *after* harvest. Pruning is done in the winter season when the vines have gone dormant. It is not a coincidence that when our lives seem to plateau or become very inactive, God chooses that season to prune us. Often times, our pruning season coincides with when He's called us into a season of rest.

Be still, and know that I am God;
I will be exalted among the nations,
I will be exalted in the earth!

— PSALM 46:10

In our stillness, we're in the prime position to allow God to trim us of the things we no longer need. In order to flourish in our next season of growth, the Lord *has* to shape us.

Pruning isn't a punishment but a way to allow the fruit of the Spirit to develop. Pruning in an earthly vineyard allows for proper air circulation, sunlight exposure, and the ability to grow new fruit that is better quality than it would have been had the vine not been pruned.

Can you see the care God has for you?

What is God trying to prune from your life?

God wants to ensure that in your next season you'll blossom as beautifully as the flowers on the trees in springtime. As part of the body of Christ, you will flower along with the other believers, making a beautiful sight in the kingdom to the angels watching above and the people walking in darkness on earth.

God is gentle in His administration and will never harm you. He wants nothing but the best for you, so do not cling tightly to the things He's asking you to surrender. Lean into His understanding, and trust that His plans are greater than the vision you desire.

> Trust in the Lord with all your heart,
> And lean not on your own understanding;
> In all your ways acknowledge Him,
> And He shall direct your paths.
>
> — PROVERBS 3:5-6

Take a moment to sit still with the Lord. Ask Him to reveal the thing(s) He wishes to prune from your life. Then ask for your trust to increase, the humility to lean into His understanding, and the will to acknowledge Him first and foremost.

A Prayer

Heavenly Father,

I thank You that You want me to continuously grow closer to You. In order to do so, I know I need to be pruned and my garden to become weed free. I understand this is a lifelong process and not one that happens overnight. Please bless me with patience in the seasons of pruning. Please give me insight to know when to surrender and when to lean on Your understanding.

In Jesus's name,

Amen.

DAY 3

Clean

You are already clean because of the word which I have spoken to you.

—JOHN 15:3

When a person cleans off grapes before eating, they quickly discover a little water goes a long way. Sometimes a person might need something like baking soda to ensure all the dirt comes off the grapes. When they dry, they shine like they're in a bright light. You're now able to enjoy the grapes with little memory that they were once covered in soil.

Why can't real life be like that? Why do we hang on to the sin that once shaped our actions but has been forgiven with Christ's sacrifice?

Jesus tells his disciples that they're already clean. I wonder if they believed Him. Did they lie awake at night recounting their sins, their mistakes, and wishing to scrub off the filth of their actions until their skin was raw?

Do you believe that you are clean? Why or why not?

Sometimes, living a certain way marks us mentally, and though we may walk in the new Way, we have trouble forgetting our past. This is a tactic of the enemy. The "mind is a playing field" and one Satan operates in frequently. The evil one wants us to remember our transgressions because if our mind is distracted by that, then we're not listening to what the Lord says.

But God operates *and* thinks differently.

> As far as the east is from the west,
> So far has He removed our transgressions from us.
>
> — PSALM 103:12

It is our flesh and the enemy's own tactics that continue to bring our past and our mistakes to the forefront. We must take every thought captive to the obedience of the Lord Jesus Christ (2 Corinthians 10:5b), because to believe anything other than what the Lord tells us is disobedience.

His sovereignty and authority make His statements and commands facts. If the Lord has pronounced us clean by our faith in Jesus Christ, since we recognized our need for a Savior and chose to follow Him, then we are clean by His say so. Nothing more needs to be said.

> The grass withers, the flower fades,
> But the word of our God stands forever.
>
> —ISAIAH 40:8

Read John 19:28-30.

God made a way for our souls to be reconciled to Him. Jesus took our sin upon Himself and made us righteous by His death on the cross. We have been cleansed by the blood of Jesus (1 John 1:7).

Jesus's ultimate sacrifice allowed us to be grafted into the vine. We were wild branches, yet now we bloom in the vineyard with the Father, the Lord Jesus Christ, and the Holy Spirit.

In order to remove the barriers that keep us from believing God's Word as truth that we are clean, we need to spend time with Him. Have you ever noticed the more time you spend with a loved one, the more you begin to have similar traits, maybe even inside jokes? There's a beauty to a long relationship where people can merely look at one another and know exactly what the other is thinking. There are no doubts in relationships like these.

This is what the Father is calling us to. When we increase our time with Him, there is no time to dwell on the enemy's lies. Instead, we begin to believe what the Father says is true, and we walk in that truth. We are His beloved, and when that knowledge is deeply rooted in our hearts, the enemy's tactics cannot withstand the love of God.

A Prayer

Heavenly Father,

Thank You for making me clean by the blood of Your Son. Please help that truth sink deep into my heart and grow roots that last my lifetime and filter to those around me. Lord, if there is anything keeping me from accepting Your Word as truth, I ask that You would remove that barrier. Pull that weed right out of my mind and throw it into the fire where it belongs. I want to believe what You say and not pay heed to the lies of the enemy. Help me renew my mind daily, hourly if needed. Please bless me with something lovely to meditate upon so that my relationship with You would strengthen.

In Jesus's name,

Amen.

DAY 4

Obedience

Abide in Me, and I in you. As the branch cannot bear fruit of itself, unless it abides in the vine, neither can you, unless you abide in Me.

—JOHN 15:4

When my oldest was a toddler, he could always be heard saying "I cannot want it" when he desired a cookie or something else he'd been refused. In his desire to be obedient, he would try and manipulate my husband and me with those big sad eyes staring at the object of his desire with the "I cannot want it." As my son grew, he stopped saying that and simply accepted that some things were not good for him. He learned to trust his father and me as wise counsel who had his best interest at heart.

Obedience is a tough thing to learn. Some of us learn quickly out of fear of making a wrong move, and some of us learn by experience, though then have to suffer the consequences of the wrong decision.

The great thing about Jesus is He told us exactly what to do and what not to do. Not every single decision is listed in the Bible. It can't be; it would be a never-ending book. However, He told us to abide in Him. This requires obedience. He goes ahead and lets us know the consequences of not abiding. The unspoken stories in between are untold because we have free will.

Will we choose Him, or will we believe our knowledge supreme and choose to march to the beat of our own drum?

In Jesus, we have the very best example of obedience.

> For as by one man's disobedience many were made sinners, so also by one Man's obedience many will be made righteous.
>
> — ROMANS 5:19

Jesus walked a path that led to death for our sins. It was not an easy road. In fact, at one point in time, His sweat was like drops of blood (Luke 22:44). Yet He did forsake His will and choose to follow the Father's. And now that we have the Holy Spirit with us, we have His power to follow in obedience as well.

> Through Him we have received grace and apostleship for obedience to the faith among all nations for His name.
>
> — ROMANS 1:5

Do you struggle with obedience? Why or why not?

____

____

____

____

Sometimes we're so gung ho to reinvent ourselves or transform ourselves that we make a plan for instant results. It's like every year when we create New Year's resolutions with the hope of seeing a new us, then forget the resolutions by the time February rolls around. The flesh is weak (Matthew 26:41). We cannot forget that we have an Advocate sent to help us.

> Nevertheless I tell you the truth. It is to your advantage that I go away; for if I do not go away, the Helper will not come to you; but if I depart, I will send Him to you.
>
> —JOHN 16:7

We have a helper we need only to call on. If we ask for His help, He will answer. God is a good Father and does not wish for any of us to struggle. If we're struggling with obedience, He will gladly help us cultivate the skill. We only need our unbelief transformed and our spirit to be willing.

A Prayer

Heavenly Father,

Please give me a heart that seeks to respond to You in immediate obedience. I do not want to struggle to obey. I don't want to obey out of misplaced fear either. I want to obey You because my love for You is so overwhelming that the only answer I can give You is "Here I am, Lord" and "Yes." Please give me a spirit that is willing, and bring my flesh into alignment.

In Jesus's name,

Amen.

DAY 5

End of the Ages

> If anyone does not abide in Me, he is cast out as a branch and is withered; and they gather them and throw them into the fire, and they are burned.
>
> —JOHN 15:6

As discussed previously, there are consequences for not abiding in Jesus. Some may see this passage as unnecessarily cruel and contradictory to who God is. However, I see the goodness of God in informing us of our choices and the corresponding consequences. If we abide in Him, we have life. If we do not, we will have death.

Honestly, it reminds me a little of the movie *The Matrix*. The protagonist, Neo, is given a choice to stay in ignorance and be ruled by the Matrix or to choose freedom. His choices are represented by a red or blue pill, but he still gets to make the choice for himself.

It is the exact same way with our Lord and Savior. We can choose life, or we can choose death.

Only the Father knows when the end harvest will come. So for now, we all still have time left to make a choice with eternal consequences.

> Let both grow together until the harvest, and at the time of harvest I will say to the reapers, "First gather together the tares and bind them in bundles to burn them, but gather the wheat into my barn."
>
> — MATTHEW 13:30

Will you be sorted as a tare or as wheat?

The problem with time is it's an illusion. When you are a teen and younger, your concept of old age could be someone who's in their twenties. You do not have the mental capacity to understand how fast birth to living in your eighties can be. Your whole life appears to be stretched before you, so time is abundant and choices are often made recklessly.

But as you age, as you grow in wisdom, you understand how fleeting time can be. That's why Jesus left behind instructions. He wanted us to be able to make choices with full understanding before time runs out.

> Behold, I tell you a mystery: We shall not all sleep, but we shall all be changed—in a moment, in the twinkling of an eye, at the last trumpet. For the trumpet will sound, and the dead will be raised incorruptible, and we shall be changed.
>
> — 1 CORINTHIANS 15:51-52

If you have been hesitant in making a choice for Jesus, please use this study to ask the questions you're holding back. God *wants* to answer you. He wants your faith to be bigger than your fear. He wants you to choose Him, but He will not force you to. Whatever your hesitation, lay it at His feet. Ask for revelation from the Holy Spirit.

But remember you may need to take a step of trust, full of faith that He is who He says He is.

> Now faith is the substance of things hoped for, the evidence of things not seen.
>
> — HEBREWS 11:1

What prevents you from fully surrendering to the Lord?

A Prayer

Heavenly Father,

I come to ask for divine revelation to illuminate exactly who You are. I ask this for the person with doubts, whoever they may be. I pray for those in my life who are filled with doubt. Please give them the answers they need. I willingly step into the gap on their behalf and ask that You help their unbelief. I pray they choose You. If I can be an instrument to sow a seed or water what has already been planted, please use me. I do not wish for any who are called to be lost. No matter what choices are made, I trust and believe that You are still a good God.

I also ask that You help assuage any doubts I may struggle on my own. Please help my unbelief and show me the way with full clarity so that I may see and hear what I need to.

In Your Son's name,

Amen.

WEEK 4

The Growing Process

DAY 1

Young Vines

VINES THAT ARE ONE TO TWO YEARS OLD ARE GENERALLY considered to be young. In this timeframe, the vinedresser is ensuring that the vines have everything they need to grow healthy and establish good trunks.

Besides the pruning process the young vines go through, they are carefully watered, protected from pests and diseases, and begin trellis training. You see, one cannot expect vines to grow in the direction they need to or to have the stability required, since their thickness is often the size of a pencil in their young stage. So they are wired to a trellis.

We, too, have been wired to a trellis, only the Holy Spirit is the gift that keeps on giving. He ensures that we are never alone, that we always have a guide, and that we are trained up in the way we need to go.

> However, when He, the Spirit of truth, has come, He will guide you into all truth; for He will not speak on His own authority, but whatever He hears He will speak; and He will tell you things to come.
>
> —JOHN 16:13

How has the Holy Spirit revealed truth to you?

Sometimes, living on an earthly plane messes with our identity. We forget we are citizens of heaven and will one day return and dwell with the Most High God. Our eyes show us a reality that we sometimes forget to view through our spiritual lens. We begin to think that our home on earth is permanent and the thing we must strive to maintain.

Our flesh must constantly be trained to submit to our spirit. This is how the Holy Spirit helps us. He reminds us of who God is in our life. Of the work Jesus did specifically for us. He's the conduit to speak God's truth over us, and He will guide us because it ultimately brings God glory.

As in the world of the vineyard, we are always wired to the Holy Spirit. Once we are baptized by Him, we have His power within us.

> And the Lord, He is the One who goes before you. He will be with you, He will not leave you nor forsake you; do not fear nor be dismayed.
>
> — DEUTERONOMY 31:8

How does knowing you're not alone help you in your faith journey?

Take the time to just sit with the Lord. Ask Him to reveal all the ways the Spirit has helped you grow from a young vine into the person you are today. Remember, we are always growing, but we can look back and take stock of what the Lord has brought us through. Remembering the acts of the Lord helps our hearts and minds to remember that we are not alone, that God answers our call and fulfills His promises.

A Prayer

Heavenly Father,

Thank You for the gift of the Holy Spirit. I know I would not be here today without Your mercy and the help of the Spirit. I ask that You would reveal some truths to me during my quiet time. Show me what I need to see at this moment in time. Open my eyes, ears, heart, and spirit. Help me to remember all of the things You've brought me through, so that my heart knows well that You are for me.

In Jesus's name,

Amen.

DAY 2

Cover Crop

A cover crop can be defined as any vegetation grown in vineyard middles and occasionally under vines without being harvested.*

As mentioned in previous days, the vinedresser takes meticulous care over his vineyard. Part of that care is using a cover crop. There are so many benefits of using a cover crop. Let me list a few that I feel are comparable to our Christian walk.

- Improves mineral fertility
- Protects against erosion
- Limits weed germination and growth
- Influences grapevine growth
- Provides firm footing†

How do these relate to our Christian walk? I'm glad you asked. We need to ensure we are getting the right "minerals" in our life.

* Pierre Helwi. "Cover Crops for Vineyard Floor Management," College of Agriculture & Life Sciences, Texas A&M University, October 2017, https://aggie-horticulture.tamu.edu/vitwine/2018/09/17/cover-crops-for-vineyard-floor-management/.
† Pierre Helwi. "Cover Crops for Vineyard Floor Management."

Taking in the Word on a daily basis provides us nutrition we cannot live without.

> So He humbled you, allowed you to hunger, and fed you with manna which you did not know nor did your fathers know, that He might make you know that man shall not live by bread alone; but man lives by every word that proceeds from the mouth of the Lord.
>
> — DEUTERONOMY 8:3

If we do not partake of "our daily bread," we will become deficient in the nutrients needed to live a righteous life. Now, I don't mean that reading the Word makes us righteous alone—only Jesus can do that. But there are tools we need to keep us on that path to drawing closer to Him and becoming more Christlike. Living by the Word of God is vital and something our cover crop provides.

Next is protecting our life against erosion. Jesus said:

> Therefore whoever hears these sayings of Mine, and does them, I will liken him to a wise man who built his house on the rock: and the rain descended, the floods came, and the winds blew and beat on that house; and it did not fall, for it was founded on the rock.
>
> — MATTHEW 7:24-25

When we have a firm foundation, we cannot be moved, cannot be shaken: "no weapon formed against you shall prosper" (Isaiah 54:17). Enemy attacks will come. Trials and tribulations of life will come in their seasons. Protecting against these and having a firm footing ensures that we are not defenseless when they happen. When our path is steady, we will be more confident when walking through the fire.

> You enlarged my path under me,
> So my feet did not slip.
>
> — PSALM 18:36

How has God recently enlarged your path? Can you think of a time He prevented You from slipping or falling off the righteous path?

____

____

____

Jesus told a lot of parables, and one memorable one is that of the wheat and tares. **Read Matthew 13:24-30**.

Our cover crop limits the amount of weeds and the damage that can be done by the weeds. God knew the enemy had sown seed just as He had, but God in His goodness provided a way for us to combat the weeds. Think of our cover crop as weed killer that will only harm it and not us.

I'm sure by now you're wondering exactly what God uses as a cover crop. First, let me tell you in an earthly vineyard, one of the favorite cover crops of choice is mustard. Yes, I said mustard.

> For assuredly, I say to you, if you have faith as a mustard seed, you will say to this mountain, "Move from here to there," and it will move; and nothing will be impossible for you.
>
> — MATTHEW 17:20B

God gave us faith that can move mountains and combat weeds. God gave us faith to supply us with the daily nutrients we need. God gave us faith that would keep our feet firmly rooted on the path and not allow them to slip. God gave us faith that ultimately helps us grow.

Read Hebrews 11.

Whose example of faith impacts you the most? Why?

One of the blessings of the Bible is that we get to read many people's shows of faith. It gives us hope that we can make it through our current trial. It gives us hope to know that we are not the only ones who may struggle with a faith crisis. Having faith doesn't mean that we will not have trials, for Jesus promised we would. What having faith means is we will trust in the One who can get us to the other side.

> Now faith is the substance of things hoped for, the evidence of things not seen.
>
> — HEBREWS 11:1

A Prayer

Heavenly Father,

Thank You for the measure of faith You have bestowed upon me. Thank You that I can increase my faith by spending time in the Word, in Your presence, and in fellowship with likeminded believers. Lord God, I ask that You increase my faith today. Show me the area(s) I am weak in so that I can submit that to You and see an increase. You are a God that would see me grow and multiply, not just physically but mentally and spiritually as well. Thank You for being a God of increase.

In Jesus's name,

Amen.

DAY 3

Fruit Set

To everything there is a season,
A time for every purpose under heaven

— ECCLESIASTES 3:1

From the time the vine is planted until it sprouts fruit can be three years. Three. Years. Now, I don't know about you, but that seems like a long time to wait for a bud to sprout and show the hard work and dedication I've put in to tending the vine. But if I've learned anything by now, it's that God's timing is not my own.

But, beloved, do not forget this one thing, that with the Lord one day is as a thousand years, and a thousand years as one day.

— 2 PETER 3:8

I often want to rush into a spiritual transformation. I had the misconception that because I'd repented and asked Jesus to forgive my sins, all my old habits would immediately fall by the wayside. Surely new habits would be as immediate as my being a new creation.

But a relationship with the Lord isn't magic-based, it's heart-based. He slowly transforms us into His likeness. He knows exactly how much change we can handle and how much time it takes for new fruit to be cultivated and to bloom. His timing is perfect, and we do *not* need to rush it.

> Patience - the state or quality of being patient; the power of suffering with fortitude; uncomplaining endurance of evils or wrongs, as toil, pain, poverty, insult, oppression, calamity, etc.*

God uses everything to build our characters (or grow our fruit, in this instance). When a vinedresser goes into his vineyard, he sees the first fruit that buds. That hard, tiny, green, and abundant fruit on the vine. It's a new creation (2 Corinthians 5:17). And just like babies who slowly develop over the years until they're grown adults, that fruit needs time to mature.

God is a compassionate God (James 5:11) and wants us to transform in the timing He has prepared for us. In a life where we rush to the next item on our checklist, slowing down can seem contrary to our goals.

Do you have trouble slowing down? Why or why not?

____

____

____

* Webster's Unabridged Dictionary (Project Gutenberg, 2009), entry for "patience," last updated June 28, 2023, https://www.gutenberg.org/cache/epub/29765/pg29765-images.html#chap16.

God is the keeper of our time and knows just exactly how much we have and when to activate a fruit, prune the fruit to enhance the flavor of one attribute, and grow another.

> Wait on the Lord;
> Be of good courage,
> And He shall strengthen your heart;
> Wait, I say, on the Lord!
>
> — PSALM 27:14

What fruit is God growing in your life currently? Why do you think He chose this one?

____

____

____

____

Read Galatians 5:22-23.

The fruit of the Spirit is something we all long to accumulate. Yet we often fail to give ourselves grace. Fruit takes three years to develop in an earthly vineyard. How much longer (or shorter, depending on *God's timing*) could it take in our spiritual lives? We have to transform our thinking and stop viewing the fruit as a checklist we have to achieve all the right marks on rather than something that is relational and deeply spiritual. Our Vinedresser is in complete control. When we submit to Him, we partner with Him, but we are still not the ones pruning and keeping up the vineyard.

A Prayer

Heavenly Father,

Thank You for Your perfect timing. In a world that is constantly giving us mixed messages about time (it's too short vs we'll die at an old age), it can be hard to view timing from Your perspective. Please give me new eyes to see the work You are doing in my vineyard. May I relish my time with You and not seek to rush the growing process. I know that the fruit has received care from You, the Vinedresser. I know Your perfect timing will allow my fruit to bloom when it is ready. Please help me to lay down my own timeline and journey with You.

In Jesus's name,

Amen.

DAY 4

Canopy Management

BEFORE THE VINEYARDS ARE BUDDING, CANOPY MANAGEMENT HAS already been discussed and planned out; from the space between rows to the vine training on trellises to the amount of shade and sunlight necessary to grow fruit.

Canopy management in our own spiritual walk is no different. Canopy management practices have three main objectives: 1) maximizing sunlight interception; 2) minimizing shading; and 3) balanced growth.*

The question really is: how can we maximize our Son-light exposure? We are called to become more and more like Christ. That's not something that is as simple as walking outside and letting the sun's rays hit our face. But there are disciplines we can put into practice that become as easy as inhaling air.

Picture yourself outside on a sunny day in the summer. (It's the perfect temperature, whatever your idea of perfect is.) Have the image in mind? Can you feel the sunlight on your skin? Do you feel

* "Pruning and Canopy Management," Western Agriculture Research Center, Montana State University, accessed June 15, 2024. https://agresearch.montana.edu/warc/guides/grapes/managing-vineyard/canopy-management.html.

the inherent joy that brings? It's no different in our faith journey when we choose to spend time with the Godhead and increase our exposure to all things Christlike.

Let's delve a little deeper into maximizing our Son-light interception. We need to fill our lives with things that matter to God. Bible studies are a great source of Son-light because we delve deeper into the Word and oftentimes with fellow believers.

> This Book of the Law shall not depart from your mouth, but you shall meditate in it day and night, that you may observe to do according to all that is written in it. For then you will make your way prosperous, and then you will have good success.
>
> —JOSHUA 1:8

Going to church is another way to get our fill of Son-light. In a church you'll often experience praise and worship, which always puts our hearts in a position to recognize God's goodness and greatness.

> I will bless the Lord at all times;
> His praise shall continually be in my mouth.
>
> — PSALM 34:1

You can also ensure that your thoughts are pointed toward God. With so much noise coming at us in the form of social media, news, commercials, infomercials, friends, and family, it's hard to get through the weeds to remember God's truth.

Read Philippians 4:8.

Why is it important to meditate on what is pure?

The other aspect important in canopy management is minimizing shading. As children of the light, we want to do our best to not dwell in the darkness. It reminds me of the scene in *The Lion King* where Mufusa takes his son, Simba, to show him every portion of the land that belongs to the lions. He tells him everything the light touches is theirs. Simba immediately asks about the shadowy places.

As new believers, we may want to figure out where that line is between light and dark and even flirt with it a little. But as we grow and experience the consequences of darkness, we learn to keep ourselves in the light.

> I beseech you therefore, brethren, by the mercies of God, that you present your bodies a living sacrifice, holy, acceptable to God, which is your reasonable service. And do not be conformed to this world, but be transformed by the renewing of your mind, that you may prove what is that good and acceptable and perfect will of God.
>
> — ROMANS 12:1-2

As believers, we need to set boundaries in our lives that keep us from giving in to the flesh. We need to heed the Holy Spirit's instruction when He gives us that nudge that lets us know without doubt that we should go the other way. After all, we *will* be tempted, but God is good and will not let us be overcome.

> No temptation has overtaken you except such as is common to man; but God is faithful, who will not allow you to be tempted beyond what you are able, but with the temptation will also make the way of escape, that you may be able to bear it.
>
> — 1 CORINTHIANS 10:13

The action of getting the right Son-light exposure and minimizing the darkness helps us complete the act of balanced growth.

There are days when I wake up and reach for my Bible and read from it. I then take time to pray to God. Then I began hygiene routines while listening to worship music. The day starts off peacefully, and I am able to handle hardships much more easily.

But there are those days when I either oversleep or for some reason end up rushing through my morning. The first thing to go is usually prayer and Bible reading time. I become more snappish by midday, and if I don't correct myself, I'm a bear by the end of the day.

Where can you carve in time to get Son-light?

____

____

____

____

____

Let me leave you with a final picture. Picture a beautiful day where the Vinedresser has entered the garden. He is pleased to see the fruit growing but sees some leaves that need to be removed for maximum Son-light exposure. In your life, those leaves looks like anger. They look like unforgiveness. They look like bitterness. They look like a prideful heart that does not see when it's wrong. Removing each of those leaves allows the fruit of the Spirit to blossom in radical ways.

We may think we need those leaves to cover us. After all, that is the exact reaction man has had since the beginning of time. But when we accepted Jesus as our Savior, we were then clothed in His righteousness. We no longer need the leaves of the flesh any longer.

> Therefore, as the elect of God, holy and beloved, put on tender mercies, kindness, humility, meekness, longsuffering; bearing with one another, and forgiving one another, if anyone has a complaint against another; even as Christ forgave you, so you also must do. But above all these things put on love, which is the bond of perfection.
>
> — COLOSSIANS 3:12-14

A Prayer

Heavenly Father,

Thank You for Your wonderful sight. That You see issues I am incapable of seeing is a blessing I thank You for. I submit myself to You for canopy management. Please pull off every leaf that is not of You and hinders my Son-light exposure. Please show me the areas where I need to remove my exposure to darkness (that are within my control) so that I can have that balanced growth of Christianity. Thank You, Father for Your gentleness in this regard.

In Jesus's Name,

Amen.

DAY 5

Weathering the Storm

> These things I have spoken to you, that in Me you may have peace. In the world you will have tribulation; but be of good cheer, I have overcome the world.
>
> —JOHN 16:33

ONE THING WE CANNOT ESCAPE IN THIS WORLD IS TRIBULATION (i.e., severe affliction). We live in a broken world where people hurt people, where natural catastrophes occur, where sin runs rampant. Jesus *knew* we would face hardships, but He did not want us to worry, because He is the Overcomer.

Still, how should we approach storms? After all, they can be detrimental to vineyards. In the earthly world, losing crops means losing out on one's livelihood. Sometimes vineyard workers have to replant in hopes they'll have enough to harvest. This is actually an area where I view our spiritual lessons veering in a different direction. For we serve the Almighty God, who has already made provision in the midst of storms.

When you pass through the waters, I will be with you;
And through the rivers, they shall not overflow you.
When you walk through the fire, you shall not be burned,
Nor shall the flame scorch you.
For I am the LORD your God,
The Holy One of Israel, your Savior.

— ISAIAH 43:2-3A

Did you know floodwaters can bring nutrients and organic matter, thus enriching the soil? If we can't avoid storms, then we should learn to see the positives. As cliché as it sounds, there are always silver linings to tribulations, thanks to our faith and hope in Jesus. Our suffering is not in vain.

Read 2 Corinthians 4:7-18. Review verses 8 and 9.

What are we, and what are we not?

When trials come our way, we have to remember to view them from the correct perspective. We must turn off the physical mindset and access the spiritual mindset.

If we live in the Spirit, let us also walk in the Spirit.

— GALATIANS 5:25

In the spiritual realm, trials and tribulation have a direct effect on our faith. There are certain character traits that develop under severe hardship and end up shining like diamonds in the aftermath.

> And not only that, but we also glory in tribulations, knowing that tribulation produces perseverance; and perseverance, character; and character, hope.
>
> — ROMANS 5:3

What is the lesson or trait you acquired from the last trial you went through? How did God refine that trait?

____

____

____

____

We fear trials and tribulations not from an eternal perspective but instinctively from a temporary, immediate standpoint. We think of the physical/mental anguish we will endure. In our humanity (flesh), we fear a trial will be more than we can bear.

It's a valid fear, and I'm not a fan of the expression "God won't put more on you than you can bear" for a few reasons. 1) It's not biblical. That exact phrase is not recorded in the Bible. 2) If that were true, why would we even need God?

What I do believe is that God walks with us in every trial. He *is* Immanuel, God with us. He gifted us with the Comforter so that He would honor His promise of never leaving us. God wants us to lean on Him during a trial and trust that He has a better plan.

> And we know that all things work together for good to those who love God, to those who are the called according to His purpose.
>
> — ROMANS 8:28

We can become bruised, battered. Our fruit can fall off the vine from storms. But that does not mean we lose our flavor as fruit would in the natural world. It doesn't mean that we are no longer part of the vine because we've taken a beating. That's a lie from the enemy. What it means is we *will* weather the storm with the help of the True Vine.

> He calms the storm,
> So that its waves are still.
>
> — PSALM 107:29

A Prayer

Heavenly Father,

I thank You for being my shelter in the storm. I know that You cannot prevent me from experiencing every hardship but that You do walk with me. For that, I thank You. Thank You for being a God of restoration and restoring what is lost in storms. Help me seek a spiritual understanding when storms come and not let my physical mindset freeze me in fear. Please be my shelter, please be my refuge in times of trouble.

In Jesus's name,

Amen.

WEEK 5

Abide

DAY 1

Abide

Abide in Me, and I in you. As the branch cannot bear fruit of itself, unless it abides in the vine, neither can you, unless you abide in Me.

—JOHN 15:4

JESUS GAVE US STRICT INSTRUCTIONS ON WHAT WE'RE SUPPOSED TO do. We're supposed to *abide.* It's the only way we'll get our spiritual nutrients from the Vine. It's the only way we can weather the storms of life (in the physical and spiritual realms).

Abide.

The word is hefty and is weighted with meaning. Let's look at the definition for a moment.

Abide - to await, remain, lodge, sojourn, dwell, continue, endure.*

---

* James Orr, ed., *International Standard Bible Encyclopedia*, entry for "abide", Bible Study Tools, Salem Media Group, 10 June 2024, https://www.biblestudytools.com/dictionary/abide/.

There is so much to unpack in the one word when we see the various meanings.

1. We are to **await**.

In one definition I saw for *await*, it used the word *expect*. Oh, how I love that imagery of us expecting Jesus to show up.

> My soul, wait silently for God alone,
> For my expectation is from Him.
>
> — PSALM 62:5

He is a God of promises and keeps His covenant, so when He says He'll do something, we can trust that one hundred percent. Hoping in the Word prevents us from spiraling into darkness. Remember, we are to minimize the spiritual darkness in the world, and expecting God to keep His promises is a perfect way to expose ourselves to Son-light.

Is there something You are expecting from God? How can You praise Him in the waiting room?

____

____

____

____

2. We are to **remain**.

A lot of Bible translations use the word *remain* instead of *abide*.

But in my opinion, they're different. Remaining gives me an image of staying.

Have you ever thrown a party and invited all of your friends and family over? Whether you're an introvert or an extrovert, you can still be exhausted by the time the party is over. But there's always that one person who remains longer than the rest.

They stay even when everyone else has already left. That's remaining. No matter what life throws at you, Jesus is asking You to keep hanging out with Him. He is the source of life, and You will perish without Him. The world will tell you lies to get you to walk away from the Source, but Jesus warns us this very thing will happen. He does not want us to be deceived and depart from Him. He is not a Man of secrets but reveals all so that we can make the right choice, the righteous choice.

3. We are to **lodge** with Jesus.

> Behold, I stand at the door and knock. If anyone hears My voice and opens the door, I will come in to him and dine with him, and he with Me.
>
> — REVELATION 3:20

The beauty of a relationship with the Creator of the universe is that He *wants* a relationship with us. He's not a distant God that we cannot talk to. Thanks to the work Jesus did on the cross, we have direct access to the Father through the Son by the power of the Spirit. The Godhead works together to have a relationship with us. We need only to confess our need of Jesus, answer the door, and dwell with Them.

When we lodge our spirit with the Godhead, we're able to walk this life with joy in our hearts. It's not that our opposition and obstacles suddenly fall away, but we will be empowered by the Spirit to get through any difficulties we may face.

> Likewise the Spirit also helps in our weaknesses. For we do not know what we should pray for as we ought, but the Spirit Himself makes intercession for us with groanings which cannot be uttered.
>
> — ROMANS 8:26

Write a prayer thanking God for dwelling with you.

____

____

____

____

Let's look at one more definition before we close for the day.

4. We are to **endure**.

In a world where sixty-second reels and YouTube shorts rule the world, endurance is not a trait everyone possesses. Our stamina is weak from constantly flitting from one thing to the next. Then again, there are times we can flex our endurance muscles by bingeing an entire series over the weekend, never moving from the couch unless food and/or bathroom breaks call to us.

In the broken world, we see people quit relationships over trivial matters or hardships they don't know how to overcome. The world needs to be pointed to the right way. *We* need to be pointed to the right way.

The Lord is asking us to continue living the way He's taught us. We are to endure, for we know hardships will come. There's not a person alive on this earth that hasn't experienced one. But with the hope of Christ, we know glory is coming and that our tears will be no more.

A Prayer

Heavenly Father,

Thank You for teaching me how to abide with You. I want to learn how to wait patiently, remain steady, and dwell with the Father, Son, and Holy Spirit. I want to endure. Help me to expect You to show up in my life and hope in Your goodness, knowing that all of these attributes will help me endure the race and make it to the finish line. Thank You for the ability to abide.

In Jesus's name,

Amen.

DAY 2

Be Present

As the Father loved Me, I also have loved you; abide in My love.

—JOHN 15:9

God doesn't just want us to be in His presence; He wants us to be present in His love. The Greek word for "present" is *endemeo,* which illustrates for one to be among one's own people. It gives me the image of being surrounded by my family in my house and how full my heart gets from those precious moments spent with the people I love the most. Can you picture it?

God wants that for us. He chose to dwell with us because He's a God of immeasurable love. We could never quantify it, but that doesn't mean we don't get to experience it.

> That Christ may dwell in your hearts through faith; that you, being rooted and grounded in love, may be able to comprehend with all the saints what is the width and length and depth and height—to know the love of Christ which passes knowledge; that you may be filled with all the fullness of God.
>
> — EPHESIANS 3:17-19

Toward the end of the year 2023, I began to sit with the Lord and ask Him what word He wanted me to focus on for the 2024 year. I've been enjoying the practice of picking a word versus making New Year's resolutions for a while now. Every year, the Lord has given me a word and my faith has stretched. My 2023 word, *joy*, seemed to be one that would carry over into the new year. I felt like it was an area that I could continue to grow in. However, in December 2023, God finally spoke and told me to, "be still."

Psalm 46:10 quickly became the verse I wanted to root myself in for 2024. Being still was something I desperately needed to learn. For me to be still likely means I have a book in hand. But even in reading, my mind is still busy as I'm living in the world of the characters. Nevertheless, my body is physically still, and it's about the only time I'm not worrying about the next task on my to-do list or worrying about something relating to adulting.

Outside of reading, being still seems foreign, to me but I *knew* I needed a slow down. So I asked God for help and to teach me. And every day, every week, and every month of the year, God showed up. I learned how to be truly present in moments with friends and family. I learned to welcome interruptions and reframe them as *divine interruptions* needed to get my attention and make sure life wasn't passing me by.

Being present in the moment is something our culture finds difficult to do. But in order to *be present* with the Lord, we need to learn to set up boundaries.

List some areas in your life you feel lack boundaries.

____

____

____

____

You may have already erected boundaries for physical stressors, relationships with friends/family who can be toxic, or even developed self-care methods to keep your mental health balanced. It's easy to do these things, because the world has many self-help books, podcasts, and influencers telling you the importance of protecting yourself.

But we don't hear a lot about creating safeguards around our spiritual life. Sure, there's the understanding that we'll attend church, we'll read our Bible if we have the time, but those things can fall into a routine and a checklist where you're still *not* fully present. Instead, we want to make sure we're carving out time that is you and the Lord and no one else.

Now I'm a huge fan of going into my closet and being alone with God. In fact, if my kids can't find me in the house, they will assume I'm in the closet praying and know to wait until I come out. I didn't turn it into anything fancy, but my brain—my *heart*—knows automatically what I'm about to do. My spirit begins to anticipate the quiet, the time with the Lord. It's different than saying a prayer at church or singing to a worship song in the car. It's just us, and nothing else has my attention. I don't allow my cell phone to be in reach—honestly, I don't even turn on the light (probably why my kids never check there first).

I've erected simple boundaries:

- no outside distractions
- talk the same time of day
- practice sitting silently so that I'm not the only one talking
- leave the closet when I feel like the conversation has truly come to an end

Now, this list doesn't mean that I'm successful in these boundaries every single time. After all, life happens. Someone could knock on my front door when I'm the only one at home. I could get a nudge from God to leave and attend to someone in my family. Whatever the case, life happens, and I give myself grace instead of shaming myself for not sticking to the boundaries. By the same token, I have adhered to these safeguards enough that everyone in my family respects my time alone with the Lord.

What are some boundaries you can put in place in order to create daily alone time with the Lord?

____

____

____

____

Here are some tips for creating boundaries.

1. Start with a few. No need to stress yourself out with a long list from the get-go, because you can always add more later.

2. Be consistent. The people in your life need to learn where your boundaries lie so they will not encroach upon them. That means you'll have to communicate kindly when they are crossed to prevent repeated incidents.
3. Figure out where your time is going. A lot of time we think an activity takes more time than it does or vice versa. Not managing our time well deters us from carving out time for the Lord. Look to see where you can realistically set aside time to be present and still with the Lord.

Boundaries are hard to set up and maintain. Not because the spirit isn't willing but because changing one habit for another takes time. You'll need to treat each day like a new day. If you didn't have time the day before, it doesn't make the next day a wash. This is where new mercies (Lamentations 3:22-23) come in and forgiveness of self. You've got this!

A Prayer

Heavenly Father,

Thank You so much for wanting to be present with me. How can it be that the Creator of the world would choose me to spend time with? Your lovingkindness is a balm to my soul, and I choose to respond in love as well. I want to spend time with You, but I don't always know how or when I can do so. Holy Spirit, please guide me in my time of reflection as I look at my calendar, to-do list, and everything else on my plate. I don't want to neglect time with You. Show me exactly when I can do this so that a habit forms and before long I *have* to show up because I know how amazing it will be to be in Your presence.

In Jesus's name,

Amen.

DAY 3

Be Held

> You shall walk after the Lord your God and fear Him, and keep His commandments and obey His voice; you shall serve Him and hold fast to Him.
>
> — DEUTERONOMY 13:4

HAVE YOU EVER HEARD OF THE SONG "JUST BE HELD" BY CASTING Crowns? It's one of those songs that touches the dark places—the valleys where we struggle to see good—and reminds you that God has you in the palm of His hand. It's about abiding. It's about God's great love for us.

Being held by God sounds marvelous to some, but to others it brings up complex emotions. Just what does it mean to *be held*? How do we surrender our wants and desires and let God have full control?

Isn't that something we're all on a journey to discover?

Last week we talked briefly about vine training and how connecting the budding vines to a trellis helps them grow strong. That connection between the branches and vine never severs. Instead, they grow strong, their fruit abounds, and we get to see the majesty and beauty of a vineyard overflowing with goodness.

Have you ever held a cluster of grapes by the stem? Those grapes are heavy, yet they don't fall off. They just are. They stay in a state of suspension, knowing they're connected until plucked off for harvest. We too can be those grape clusters and trust the connection we've been developing with the Lord.

You may be like a baby in faith, having just come to the revelation of Jesus Christ and who He is. That's okay. You're still connected and your branch will grow in strength. If you've been walking alongside Jesus for a while, your branch has already grown and developed the necessary muscles to maintain your connection to the True Vine. However, that doesn't mean you're done growing.

Wherever we fall on the spectrum of growth, Jesus is there. *Jesus is there*. Sit in that revelation for a moment.

What helps you understand that Jesus is always with You?

____

____

____

____

Let's talk about some practical tips for learning how to lean into Jesus and just be held.

1. Eradicate the fear.

Fear is a pesky thing that keeps on coming back, especially if you feed into it. If you don't transform your thoughts to meditate on the good, fear will grow. But when you cut off the thoughts and remind yourself of what God has done for you, fear stops at the mighty power of God.

Now, that's not to say it will be gone forever. We *are* human and thus react in the natural way humans do. But we can learn to fight fear so that we won't succumb to it the next time our paths cross.

**Please note that I'm not referring to a fear that stems from depression and anxiety or other mental health issues. Sometimes those can only be addressed by a medical professional in the capacity they deem best. If you feel that you are suffering from mental health issues, please contact a professional.*

I find having a verse at the ready often helps combat fear.

> Peace I leave with you, My peace I give to you; not as the world gives do I give to you. Let not your heart be troubled, neither let it be afraid.
>
> —JOHN 14:27

Having a verse to repeat when your mind is tempted to spiral can pull you out of the darkness. You can get a phone wallpaper with the verse, put it on a sticky note and place where you're most likely to see it, or just practice memorization so that it will be at the ready. Don't forget you can seek the Spirit for a verse as well.

2. Hold onto His Word.

One issue I've seen in my own life is that I sometimes believe something I've heard or seen over what is in the Bible. Not because I have doubts but because the worldly input is so loud that it drowns out the truths of the Bible. Once I realize this is the case, I take a moment to pray and ask God to remove the lies built up in my mind.

Living in this world requires a lot of maintenance on our part. We have to be willing to do the work of prayer, Bible study, communing with likeminded people, etc. Without spiritual disciplines, the truth will get choked off by the cares of the world.

> Then Jesus said to those Jews who believed Him, "If you abide in My word, you are My disciples indeed. And you shall know the truth, and the truth shall make you free."
>
> —JOHN 8:31-32

3. Hold on to the promise of eternity.

What we do on this earth matters, without a doubt. But what we do on this earth is temporary. How we live, how we eat, what we wear are all temporary concerns. It doesn't negate their importance, but we should never put the temporary over the eternal. We have hope in Jesus's return. In a promise of heavenly bodies, no tears, no sorrow (Revelation 21:4). We will be rejoicing with all nations and angels and heavenly beings with God among us.

That is a hope that will carry us through trials: on mountain tops and in valleys. We have a God who cares not only for our present but for all of our tomorrows.

> Fight the good fight of faith, lay hold on eternal life, to which you were also called and have confessed the good confession in the presence of many witnesses.
>
> — 1 TIMOTHY 6:12

List the ways you have been or are currently being held by the Lord.

___

___

___

A Prayer

Today, write a prayer to God thanking Him for the ways He's held you over the years. Thank Him for the ways You've submitted to Him and allowed Him to hold you. Let the Spirit guide you in your prayer time. If you get stuck, remember the way Jesus taught the disciples how to pray (Matthew 6:9-13).

DAY 4

Remain as One

> I do not pray for these alone, but also for those who will believe in Me through their word; that they all may be one, as You, Father, are in Me, and I in You; that they also may be one in Us, that the world may believe that You sent Me.
>
> —JOHN 17:20-21

THE BIBLE SHOWS US MANY VERSES TALKING ABOUT THE BENEFITS of being united in the body of Christ and with the holy Trinity. It makes sense because Christ Himself modeled this.

Read Matthew 3:13-17.

When Jesus was baptized—and as when anyone confesses their faith in the Lord—the Spirit descended upon Him. When I confessed my faith in Jesus, I later was baptized. Having been blessed with the gift of the Spirit, my days are filled with the Father, Son, and Holy Spirit. I am not alone in my walk. In praying to God, through Jesus, by the power of the Spirit, I'm remaining as one with them.

It's the same walk Jesus modeled for us and the same prayer He prayed in John 17 for His disciples and those who would later come to belief. Unity in the body of Christ is vital to our lives.

> For as the body is one and has many members, but all the members of that one body, being many, are one body, so also is Christ. For by one Spirit we were all baptized into one body—whether Jews or Greeks, whether slaves or free—and have all been made to drink into one Spirit.
>
> —1 CORINTHIANS 12:12-13

There are so many dissensions in the body right now. But instead of fixating on the whole part, let us first examine ourselves. Do we have times where we come together with other believers for the express purpose of worshiping God as one (Hebrews 10:25)? Do we take steps to walk through hardships together with other believers, both theirs and our own (2 Corinthians 1:4)? Are we giving preference to each other and walking in love (Romans 12:10-13)? Once we've done the work on ourselves, next we can focus on the body.

There are many ways we can maintain peace within the body of believers. We shouldn't focus on how we are different but on how we all believe in the One True God and are attached to the True Vine. That is something to celebrate.

But unity within the body isn't the only unity we experience. We get to experience unity with the Father, Son, and Holy Spirit. After all, isn't unity the whole point of abiding in Jesus? Remaining in Him? We are to unite ourselves in such a way that we can't tell where Jesus ends and we begin. Our reactions should stem from all the time we've spent dwelling with the Lord. When people interact with us, something about us should point to Jesus.

Sometimes we can't take stock of ourselves accurately and know without a doubt that our lives profess our faith. So your homework—really the only homework in this book—is to find a trusted friend. Ask them what they see in you that points to Jesus. I guarantee you'll be surprised by their answer, and I hope, humbled and honored.

> But he who is joined to the Lord is one spirit with Him.
>
> —1 CORINTHIANS 6:17

One of the blessings in remaining one with the Father, Son, and Spirit is that the hard work is not done by us. It's completed simply by accepting Jesus as our Savior and being sealed by the Holy Spirit.

> In Him you also trusted, after you heard the word of truth, the gospel of your salvation; in whom also, having believed, you were sealed with the Holy Spirit of promise.
>
> —EPHESIANS 1:13

When you are *sealed*, you are marked as belonging to God. The works of the Spirit confirm your belief in Jesus. You *are* one. But like every relationship, there is more work to be done. The work of communicating. Taking time to sit and be alone with them shows that the relationship is of the utmost importance to you. Like you would make plans to meet up with a friend and catch up on each other's lives, you need to make plans to sit and check in with the Lord. The Great I AM seeks our company and is always ready to open the lines of communication in ways we've never imagined.

> Call to Me, and I will answer you, and show you great and mighty things, which you do not know.
>
> —JEREMIAH 33:3

What are some ways you can keep the lines of communication open with the Lord?

Pray for the Body

Today, write a prayer for the body of Christ. It can be specific to your church community, small group, Bible study participants, or even those far away whom you've never met before. Let the Spirit guide you to pray for those who have professed with their lips that Jesus is Lord.

DAY 5

Wait for Him

> So Christ was offered once to bear the sins of many. To those who eagerly wait for Him He will appear a second time, apart from sin, for salvation.
>
> —HEBREWS 9:28

THERE'S GOOD NEWS COMING. ACCEPTING JESUS AS OUR SAVIOR and being saved from our sins is a gift we can never earn. It's offered freely by God to all who believe in His Son. But the gifts don't stop there. Jesus will return and gather all of us, from *all* nations, to the place He's been preparing. That is radical news. That is hope. That is what we're all eagerly waiting for.

> In My Father's house are many mansions; if it were not so, I would have told you. I go to prepare a place for you. And if I go and prepare a place for you, I will come again and receive you to Myself; that where I am, there you may be also.
>
> —JOHN 14:2-3

As I've matured in my faith, I've gone from impatiently waiting for Jesus to wondering how I can wait well. To explain further, I live with chronic pain. I always hurt and have been hurting for a couple of decades now. What used to be one issue giving me grief is now a multitude. On top of that, I suffer from depression and anxiety because of the chronic pain. The idea of getting a heavenly body and not experiencing any suffering is something I often impatiently wait for. I *want* the pain to stop, and some days when it feels unbearable, I *need* the pain to stop.

But God is with me and gets me through those dark times and reminds me of hope. So now, in my fourth decade on this earth, I wonder, how can I wait well?

> But those who wait on the Lord
> Shall renew their strength;
> They shall mount up with wings like eagles,
> They shall run and not be weary,
> They shall walk and not faint.
>
> — ISAIAH 40:31

What does waiting well for Jesus's return mean to you?

____

____

____

____

____

Read Matthew 25:1-13. Pick your favorite commentary and read what the parable means.

In the parable of the wise and foolish virgins we get a picture of what it's like to wait for Jesus. The wise virgins brought not only their lights but also oil to refill their lamps when they went down. So the first criteria for waiting well is to shine our light.

> You are the light of the world. A city that is set on a hill cannot be hidden.
>
> — MATTHEW 5:14

We are to shine for the world because it's in darkness. As Christ's ambassadors (2 Corinthians 5:20), we are to be that light in the world. We are to show the world what living in the light looks like.

Some of us do this well. We're not afraid to be in the spotlight, and we do not let others' opinions keep us from being exactly who God created us to be. Others of us need to embrace the fullness of who we are in Christ and walk in that freedom. Remember, your uniqueness has a purpose and was designed by God.

But if you refer back to the wise virgins, shining isn't all that's required. We must also refuel our light! There are a myriad of ways we can do this, but I think one we shouldn't forget is to rest.

> So the people rested on the seventh day.
>
> — EXODUS 16:30

God built a day of rest into our week, and we should not be so obstinate as to believe that it isn't necessary. If God saw fit to make a commandment about rest, then it's not an idle ideal. It's vital to replenish our souls in a world that would drain us. We're drained by the wages of sin, drained by the hurt of the world and the compassion that rises up in response, we're drained in pouring out to others. Doing good does not come from an unending well within us but from the True Vine. If we do not rest in Him and take a moment for the Spirit to administer to us, our light will diminish. Not to mention the virgins who thought they did not need oil were likened unto someone who is foolish.

The last thing the parable teaches us is to watch.

> Watch therefore, for you know neither the day nor the hour in which the Son of Man is coming.
>
> — MATTHEW 25:13

We shouldn't walk this life as if we have all the time in the world to live a life for Christ; we should walk with a posture of vigilance.

If you knew your life would end in the next month, would you feel you have waited well?

____

____

____

____

This isn't a question I want you to answer right away. This is a question that requires time spent with the Lord. Only He can tell you if you're on the right path or need to veer onto a different one. He can tell you if you've been shining your light exactly as He made you to or if you need to refuel. This question is merely to give you direction in your quiet time with the Father, Son, and Holy Spirit.

If you feel convicted, please do not sit in a place of shame. That's not what God wants; that's a lie from the enemy. What God wants is your full attention and for you to let Him be the potter and you the clay. God is merciful, compassionate, and loving. He does not hand out shame nor guilt.

What was your biggest takeaway from this week?

___

___

___

___

___

WEEK 6

Vineyard Benefits

DAY 1

Ask and Receive

If you abide in Me, and My words abide in you, you will ask what you desire, and it shall be done for you.

—JOHN 15:7

Have you ever seen a baby play with a cardboard box and be happy? Or better yet, discover that banging a wooden spoon on a pot makes the most joyful noise? It doesn't matter that you've bought your child the latest toys; they will always go for the simple. It's not because they're shunning what you have to offer, but the world is so complex that the simple can fascinate a child.

But as we age, we move from that childlike innocence and awe to a more jaded realism that can cripple us in the blessings department. And I don't mean that we stop receiving blessings, but oftentimes, we stop asking for them.

We learn to settle.

Settling can stem from living through too many trials and tribulations or being jaded by the sin running rampant in the world. Settling can stem from insecurity or being unable to identify our worth as a child of God. Whatever the reason, we stop asking God for blessings.

We believe that being clothed, fed, and having a roof over our heads is enough.

And it is. After all, Paul talks about being content in Philippians 4:11-12. But being content is different from settling. Settling indicates fear. Fear of not being enough. Fear of not being deserving. Fear.

And God is the absence of fear.

> There is no fear in love; but perfect love casts out fear, because fear involves torment.
>
> — 1 JOHN 4:18A

What prevents you from asking God for more?

____

____

____

____

In John 15, Jesus tells His disciples that abiding with Him comes with benefits. Essentially, they can ask and receive.

> Ask, and it will be given to you; seek, and you will find; knock, and it will be opened to you. For everyone who asks receives, and he who seeks finds, and to him who knocks it will be opened.
>
> — MATTHEW 7:7-8

This is not a magic-genie type of situation. Believers in Christ won't get a lamp to rub and have unlimited requests. This is one born of a true relationship. One between a Father and His children. When you have experienced the love of a parent who wants nothing but the best for you, you *know* you can ask for something, and if your earthly parent is able to and believes it to be best, receive.

It is the same premise with the Lord but better in so many ways. For one, God is all-knowing. He knows exactly what you want before you ask for it. And if you have been abiding in Him, then you know He abides in you. Therefore, your desires are born from His will. You want to please Him and He desires the same. And giving to His children pleases Him.

I think many of us are afraid of being selfish and self-seeking, so we keep quiet. But when you are asking for something that falls in His will, how can your request be selfish?

Let me give you an example.

Since my children were little, I have prayed that they would come to know the Lord. It's my deepest desire that they will grow into men of God. Men who are after the Lord's own heart and seek Him with all of theirs. That is not a selfish prayer. It is one that comes from me spending time with God, seeing the benefits in our relationship, and wishing someone else would be able to experience the same love I have. God and I are one in this accord. He wants my children to choose to follow Him more than I can fully comprehend. This desire shows how much I have chosen to abide in Him.

By the same token, the prayers I've had that *were* selfish and self-seeking fell by the wayside. It's because God was able to show me the very nature of those prayers as I spent time with Him. I was able to repent and let those dreams go. But I know letting those desires go means that something better is in store. Something I have yet to see or comprehend, because I serve a God that is that good.

> Now to Him who is able to do exceedingly abundantly above all that we ask or think, according to the power that works in us, to Him be glory in the church by Christ Jesus to all generations, forever and ever. Amen.
>
> — EPHESIANS 3:20-21

Is there a desire that You need to let go and let the Lord replace with His desires?

How can we ensure that what we ask falls in the Father's will?

1. We ask.

The one thing I'm sure to do when I am asking God a big ask (you know, that move you're desiring, the new home, that promotion, or maybe something like a big purchase item) is to let Him know I want to remain in His will.

> Your kingdom come.
> Your will be done
> On earth as it is in heaven.
>
> — MATTHEW 6:10

When Jesus taught the Lord's Prayer, He taught us how to remain in the Lord's will. Simply acknowledging that You desire His plan over your own keeps your heart in a humble posture.

2. We abide.

After all, this is the whole point of this study—to learn what it means to abide in the True Vine. We let Him lead, we let the Spirit guide, and we will come to the conclusion that is spiritual versus flesh-guided.

3. We wait.

Last week we talked about waiting well, and with prayer, this is usually the next step. We wait on the Lord's answer and on His timing.

Keeping these simple acts will help us seek God's will above our own but also keep the line of communication open between us so that we can ask and receive.

Prayer points

Spend time writing out in a journal what you want to ask the Lord for. Don't worry about how small or big the ask is. Ask, knowing Your Father loves you more than you can fathom and wants great things for you.

DAY 2

Increased

> By this My Father is glorified, that you bear much fruit; so you will be My disciples.
>
> —JOHN 15:8

One of the benefits of being in the vineyard is watching the fruit multiply. The ability to wander row by row and see the fruit of your labor is something that a sower takes pride in.

God has given us the nutrients needed for us to increase in faith, spiritual disciplines, and all that He is trying to teach us. This increase is a blessing from God and shows us part of His nature. Scripture tells us that God is a God of increase.

As Paul said in 1 Corinthians 3:6:

> I planted, Apollos watered, but God gave the increase.

I think when we hear the word *increase* we assume a spatial difference will be visible to the naked eye, but in the Corinthians verse, but "increase" translates the Greek word *auxano* which means "to grow."*

Being saved from our sins by Jesus's sacrifice makes salvation such a beautiful gift. It's one we're forever grateful for. It also fills our hearts with love for a God who provided that sacrifice even though we were underserving. Because of this, we yearn to be closer and to seek Him more. Our hearts desire more of Him. Our salvation moves us into a posture of sanctification.

Our whole spiritual experience is one of growth, a.k.a. increase. It is not a material gains situation, where loving God will make our income increase in a way that can only be attributed to Him. But it is one where our hearts turn more and more toward Him and our faith walk looks more and more like He designed from the very beginning.

> May the Lord give you increase more and more,
> You and your children.
> May you be blessed by the Lord,
> Who made heaven and earth.
>
> — PSALM 115:14-15

In this psalm, "increase" comes from the Hebrew word *yacaph*. One of the definitions of this word is "to do more, do again."†

Read Matthew 14:13-21.

As you can see, Jesus met the needs of the five-thousand-plus people in attendance. They were hungry for spiritual food, but He did not forget their physical need as well. He gave an increase. It's why Matthew 6:25-34 encourages us not to worry.

---

* New Testament Greek Lexicon – King James Version," entry for "auxano," Bible Study Tools, Salem Media Group, accessed June 15, 2024, https://www.biblestudytools.com/lexicons/greek/kjv/auxano.html.

† "A Hebrew and English Lexicon of the Old Testament," entry for "yacaph," accessed June 17, 2024, Bible Study Tools, https://www.biblestudytools.com/lexicons/hebrew/kjv/yacaph.html.

Do you doubt that God wants to take care of your needs? If so, why?

When your spiritual needs need to be met, God knows and already has a plan worked out to meet those needs. He knows because He's the master Vinedresser. He's been tending to you since long before you sprouted and bore flowers, then fruit, then *abundant* fruit.

> I have come that they may have life, and that they may have it more abundantly.
>
> —JOHN 10:10B

Our abundance is not meant to be kept to ourselves. We are to use it to increase the whole body of Christ and not just one member.

Read 2 Corinthians 9:8-11.

Have you ever thought about the people who supplied the loaves and fishes for Jesus to multiply? What joy they must have felt knowing their meager offering was used to supply all in attendance. That is the beauty of being part of the body and being used by God.

How can you be a blessing to someone this week?

____

____

____

____

This week, I'd like to do something different. Instead of a prayer, instead of journaling, let's memorize a scripture.

Memory Verse

> Blessed is the man who trusts in the Lord,
> And whose hope is the Lord.
> For he shall be like a tree planted by the waters,
> Which spreads out its roots by the river,
> And will not fear when heat comes;
> But its leaf will be green,
> And will not be anxious in the year of drought,
> Nor will cease from yielding fruit.
>
> —JEREMIAH 17:7-8

DAY 3

One

> Therefore let that abide in you which you heard from the beginning. If what you heard from the beginning abides in you, you also will abide in the Son and in the Father.
>
> — 1 JOHN 2:24

In the beginning, God created man and woman in His image (Genesis 1:26-27), and we were to dwell with Him. That has always been the plan, despite man's sin creating a fallen world. For the past month and a half, we have discussed how important it is to abide in God's Word and create a relationship with Him that our sin attempted to tear apart.

Thank the Lord, He knew better and created a way for us to be reconciled to Him through the blood of Jesus. The relationship we now have allows us to be one and have God dwell with us.

> And the Word became flesh and dwelt among us, and we beheld His glory, the glory as of the only begotten of the Father, full of grace and truth.
>
> —JOHN 1:14

We live in a world that likes to mark our differences as something that sets us apart from one another, as if we're in strict competition. Who can be the best, who can accrue the most accolades the quickest, etc. But God teaches us a different way.

> Let nothing be done through selfish ambition or conceit, but in lowliness of mind let each esteem others better than himself. Let each of you look out not only for his own interests, but also for the interests of others.
>
> — PHILIPPIANS 2:3-4

We are the branches stemming from the True Vine. We are one, yet many parts. Individual, yet united. We do not move to elevate ourselves but to elevate the body.

Read 1 Corinthians 12:12-17.

Why do you supposed God created us to be one? What is the importance in being unified?

____

____

____

____

There are many Bible verses that talk about the body of Christ and how we are to behave. But let's go back to the very beginning, to the garden of Eden, Genesis 1, when everything was good in God's eyes.

We were meant to be in harmony with one another, to complement one another, to dwell together with God. Just because man has sinned, and sinned some more, doesn't negate God's original plan for us. That is something we have to constantly remind ourselves of.

Instead, we need to search for moments to be together as the body.

> And let us consider one another in order to stir up love and good works, not forsaking the assembling of ourselves together, as is the manner of some, but exhorting one another, and so much the more as you see the Day approaching.
>
> — HEBREWS 10:24-25

Besides coming together as a body of believers, we also need to come together with the Father, Son, and Holy Spirit. Time spent with them will only enrich every area of our lives as previously discussed.

Prayer Points

Sit with the Lord and ask Him to show you how you can increase your time spent with a body of believers. Maybe you already do so—the ask Him how you can maximize that time and be fully present. He will answer You in His perfect timing.

DAY 4

Valued

Look at the birds of the air, for they neither sow nor reap nor gather into barns; yet your heavenly Father feeds them. Are you not of more value than they?

— MATTHEW 6:26

BECAUSE THE WORLD IS RIFE WITH SIN, EACH OF US HAS A STORY OF a time we felt less than. I grew up in a single-parent household and felt the absence of my absentee parent acutely. Surely there was something wrong with me, something I'd done to make them go away.

This was the mindset I held way into my twenties, and because I believed those lies so intricately, I committed my own sins of my own volition. Had I known my worth, had I known how God sees me, I would have chosen differently.

Read Psalm 139.

Verse fourteen is one that has been shared by more people than we can count. Not only that, but you can find many items of apparel with those words or even knickknacks to decorate your home with. And it's not because the saying is cliché. Not at all. That verse hits home because it resonates so deeply with people worldwide that it must be shared over and over. Each share comes with the hope that a reader will believe the words to be true.

The Hebrew word *yare** from verse fourteen does not mean *fear* as in to be scared of something. In this instance, it speaks to being in awe of or holding deep honor and respect for. What would it mean for your heart, your soul, to believe that you are "fearfully and wonderfully made"?

We need a value recalibration. Only, we won't seek the world's definition but the Lord's.

> But God demonstrates His own love toward us, in that while we were still sinners, Christ died for us.
>
> — ROMANS 5:8

Our worth does not come from being free from sin, because as the verse above alludes to, we were *not* sin free. Our value comes from God's love, which we can never quantify.

> Behold what manner of love the Father has bestowed on us, that we should be called children of God!
>
> — 1 JOHN 3:1A

We are His children, and that is all that is needed to give us value. In a world that requires something of us in order to be counted worthy, it is absolutely refreshing to encounter a God who wants nothing more than for us to surrender wholly to Him.

I can vividly picture myself resting my head on Jesus's knee and Him stroking my hair. The trust in submitting to Him, the love He

---

* "A Hebrew and English Lexicon of the Old Testament," entry for "yare," Bible Study Tools, Salem Media Group, accessed June 15, 2024, https://www.biblestudytools.com/lexicons/hebrew/kjv/yare.html.

bestows on us—it's a beautiful picture of the relationship between the church and Savior.

Take a minute to close your eyes and ask Jesus to give you a picture of what it looks like when He values you. After all, we are all created differently, so my picture may not resonate with you because He has a different one in mind for you.

Write that picture down.

____

____

____

____

> The Lord your God in your midst,
> The Mighty One, will save;
> He will rejoice over you with gladness,
> He will quiet you with His love,
> He will rejoice over you with singing.
>
> — ZEPHANIAH 3:17

Because He values us, He will care for us. He will meet our needs (physical, spiritual, mental). He will increase our fruit so that our spirit will be fed in a way that is unique to each of us.

He cares for you—never forget that fact.

Read Psalm 23.

How does God care for you?

____

____

____

____

Let's end with a prayer.

A Prayer

Heavenly Father,

Thank You for seeing value in me before I could recognize my own worth. Thank You for a love that is all-encompassing. Without it, I would be lost. Today I ask that You would remove any barriers I have to accepting that You made me "fearfully and wonderfully." May I experience new ways that reaffirm how You see me. Please demolish the lies I've been believing about myself, so that I will not see myself as unworthy ever again.

In Jesus's name,

Amen.

DAY 5

The Father's Will

> No longer do I call you servants, for a servant does not know what his master is doing; but I have called you friends, for all things that I heard from My Father I have made known to you.
>
> —JOHN 15:15

ONE OF THE THINGS REPEATED IN JOHN 15 IS HOW TO ABIDE IN THE Lord, which honestly, is nothing but doing the Father's will. One of the first things any believer wants to know is *Am I doing God's will?* We want to ensure we're walking the path He's laid out for us. Sometimes it's fear of messing up and deviating from the path. Sometimes it's because we've purposely taken a fork in the road and we want to find our way back. Whatever the reason, knowing God's will is vital to the believer.

In John 15:15, Jesus makes known to the disciples that He has told them everything the Father made known to Him. By extension, we have been blessed to have a blueprint (the Bible) left behind for us to also know the will of the Lord.

I'm not talking about the mysteries of God. I will discuss that later. But I'm talking about the moral road God wishes us to follow.

Here are some Scriptures to look up:

- Proverbs 3:5-6
- Micah 6:8
- Matthew 6:10
- Ephesians 5:15-21
- 1 Thessalonians 4:3
- 1 Thessalonians 5:16-18
- 1 Timothy 2:3-4
- 1 Peter 2:15-17
- 2 Peter 3:8-9

Based on the above scriptures, what is the will of God?

____

____

____

____

God wants us to believe in His Son, repent and receive salvation, and live a holy life (Romans 12:2). It's a walk that naturally shifts from inward to outward as we continue to abide in Him, soak in His Word, and be in communion with the Father, Son, and Holy Spirit.

Doing the Father's will is an everyday choice, and sometimes a by-the-second decision. We choose righteousness, we choose to believe in His promises no matter what the world shows us, we choose to walk in faith.

> Now the just shall live by faith...
>
> — HEBREWS 10:38A

We need to live by faith (Hebrews 11:1-3) each and every day. Studying the Word is doing the Father's will. Talking to Him each day is doing His will. Listening to the Spirit and not grieving Him is doing the Father's will (Ephesians 4:30).

The Father's will could be an entirely new Bible study, so forgive me for purposely remaining brief on the subject. However, I do want to give you enough material so that you can sit with these scriptures, with this idea in your own time as the Holy Spirit guides you further into revelation. Because although the Bible expresses God's will in many areas, there are things still unknown to us.

> It is the glory of God to conceal a matter,
> But the glory of kings is to search out a matter.
>
> — PROVERBS 25:2

The mysteries of God are the unspoken principles He has yet to share with us. Those are the characteristics that are unique to you and you alone. Those are the unknowns that God wishes you to seek Him first in. I can't reveal them to you, because that is not my place. But I think that is the beauty of these mysteries. God wants a relationship with us, and that involves communication. If we do not seek Him (communicate via prayer) then our communication skills will be severely lacking on our part.

Abiding in God is keeping the lines of communication open so that when He is ready to reveal new knowledge to you, you are open to receiving His instructions.

Homework

Sit with the Lord and ask Him if there is any area of your life that is not submitted to Him and in His will. Keep an open mind, an open heart, so that You will have ears to hear and eyes to see what His perfect will is.

Please remember, if you feel any shame for not being in His will, that is a tactic of the enemy. God does not condemn or shame (Romans 8:1). Convict, yes. Shame, no. Let Him guide you in repentance and onto a new, righteous path. He will tell you exactly what you need to know when you need to know it in a gentle, loving matter (1 John 1:9).

WEEK 7

Bear Fruit

DAY 1

Abide in my Love

As the Father loved Me, I also have loved you; abide in My love.

—JOHN 15:9

JESUS DOESN'T ONLY WANT US TO ABIDE IN HIM BUT ALSO TO remain in His love. It brings to mind a beautiful picture of a child resting in their Father's arms, fully secure, fully content, at peace, knowing that all is right.

God wants us at peace. He wants us secure in His love because He knows love is the answer. After all, God is love.

Read 1 John 4:7-21.

1. How does one know God?

2. How was God's love manifested toward us?

3. How is God's love perfected in us?

4. How do we know that we abide in Him?

The love spoken of in John 15:9 is from the Greek *agape*, which is the highest form of love there is. It is the love of God toward man and the love man has toward God.

This love is sacrificial, as we see in 1 John 4:10. Jesus came to be a sacrifice so that we could be reconciled to the Father. It's a love that means we lay aside our desires and seek the wellness of our brothers and sisters in Christ.

Read 1 Corinthians 13:4-8.

What is love?

___

___

___

___

This type of love has been modeled for us by Christ, and He asks that we love each other as well (John 13:35). But abiding in His love is not all Jesus says on the subject.

> If you keep My commandments, you will abide in My love, just as I have kept My Father's commandments and abide in His love.
>
> —JOHN 15:10

Jesus asks us to keep the commandments. What commandments, you ask? **Read Mark 12:29-31.**

What commandments is Jesus asking us to abide in?

Loving God with all we have and loving others as we'd love ourselves are fulfillments of the commandments. When we seek to love others as 1 Corinthians 13 describes, we are seeking to do God's will and abide in His love. His love flows through us and fills us up. We are then to pour out His love to others. It's a conduit that keeps on going as long as we continue to abide in Him and He in us.

Prayer Points

Grab a notecard, a journal, or use the space below. Write down a couple of ways you can love God, love yourself, and love others. Let the Holy Spirit guide you in this and have fun with it! Love makes the world go round.

DAY 2

Joy

> These things I have spoken to you, that My joy may remain in you, and that your joy may be full.
>
> —JOHN 15:11

ONE OF THE THINGS I LOVE ABOUT GOD IS HOW HE LOOKS OUT for us in totality. He doesn't just want us to repent and live a sanctified life. He wants us to have joy!

> For the kingdom of God is not eating and drinking, but righteousness and peace and joy in the Holy Spirit.
>
> —ROMANS 14:17

What an amazing look at His character—one that exudes joy and love and hope to all who would look toward Him for the meaning of life. It's not in worldly gains or strictly in self-love. It's loving God, loving others, living an abundant life.

What does joy mean to you?

Read John 16:16-24.

God offers an everlasting joy that is rooted in our belief in Jesus, the True Vine, whom we abide in. This joy is that we have been saved from our sins through the loving sacrifice Jesus gifted us. This joy is in the peace we feel knowing we are not alone because the Holy Spirit has been sent to us. This joy is knowing that one day, Jesus will return and there will be no more tears (Revelation 21:4). This is a joy that will see us through various trials, because they are coming.

> My brethren, count it all joy when you fall into various trials, knowing that the testing of your faith produces patience. But let patience have its perfect work, that you may be perfect and complete, lacking nothing.
>
> —JAMES 1:2-4

How is it possible to maintain joy during a difficult time in your life?

One of the trials of being human and not divine is that our perspective is so limited. It's been shaped by our past experiences, by our dealings with others (good or bad), and by who we are inherently. Add in the trial of living in a fallen world where some sin gleefully and without repentance—nor do they care how their actions affect others—and our view shrinks even more inward.

Read Matthew 14:22-33.

The disciples were in a literal storm, but at the beckoning of Jesus and with a step of faith, Peter was able to walk on water. While his focus remained on Jesus, he wasn't bothered by the storm.

If Jesus is calling you to something greater than the storm you're in, you can rest assured that the storm is literal background noise at this point. That doesn't mean the winds aren't scary; we're human after all. Our emotions *will* respond to the stressors in our life. It's what we do with those emotions that gets us into trouble or keeps us aligned with God.

Journal idea

Do you like to journal? If so, creating a gratitude journal can be life-changing. Counting your blessings shifts your mindset and allows your view of goodness to widen.

If you don't like to journal, consider counting your blessings in the way God gifted you. If you're creative, perhaps you can sketch some of the blessing in your life, or maybe you prefer poetry. How about creating a photo album of blessings on your phone or writing a song to the Lord? If that's not in your wheelhouse, you can curate a playlist with songs that make you grateful.

Whatever your way, keep track of the blessings the Lord has given you. I'm sure the Holy Spirit will lead you on a personal journey.

DAY 3

Love Others

This is My commandment, that you love one another as I have loved you. Greater love has no one than this, than to lay down one's life for his friends.

—JOHN 15:12-13

BEING PART OF THE VINEYARD MEANS THAT WE ARE NOT ALONE IN this life. We have built-in community to celebrate the ups and mourn the downs with us. When we love, God moves. When God moves, change happens.

The sacrificial love of laying down your wants and desires and choosing another's wants and desires above your own is powerful. You can see this kind of love in every relationship under the sun.

As a mother, I know without a doubt that I would die for my children. And though that's the ultimate sacrifice, it doesn't mean that I don't sacrifice on a daily basis. I may choose to have a cell phone that's older because my kid wants to participate in a sport or activity. I'm willing to let go of my wants to help them discover a potential talent or just enjoy life to the full.

In our marriage, my husband and I regularly sacrifice for one another. I absolutely adore country music, and my husband would rather listen to anything but that genre. Yet when my favorite country music artist came to our state, he was right there beside me as I sang to every song. He laid aside his distaste for the music for a moment to see me happy. And I've never forgotten that moment, because it's one I felt his love acutely.

> A new commandment I give to you, that you love one another; as I have loved you, that you also love one another. By this all will know that you are My disciples, if you have love for one another.
>
> —JOHN 13:34-35

When we choose to love as it's listed in 1 Corinthians 13, the world takes notice. I've seen people start to research who God is because of the love they were shown by His children. I've seen wounded people let down their guard because of the love shown by believers. Love is powerful. Love is life-changing. Love laid down His life for mine.

What was the last sacrifice you made to make someone else happy? How did they respond? How did you feel afterwards?

___

___

___

___

We live in a climate with political unrest, with crimes committed on a daily basis, with people flaunting a sinful lifestyle. It can be overwhelming to us, and when people are overwhelmed, they often react badly. But we are not called to judge another (Matthew 7:1-6) for we are *not* God and are ill-equipped to discern a person's motives (their heart). We are simply (and not so simply) called to love.

I think in our human understanding, we believe that if we love another, that automatically means we agree with everything they stand for. And that's just not the case. Even God does not agree with every single action you've done in the past. But because of His Son, God will give us clean slates and not remember our sins.

Read Romans 12:9-21. 1 Peter 4:7-10.

What are some of the ways we can love others?

___

___

___

___

When we love others, we fulfill the commandments given in Exodus 20 that deal with relationships with others. When we stop to think how we would want to be treated in a situation, we're able to think before acting. When we remember that people are God's creation and therefore automatically worthy of love, then we pause before letting our emotions take us to a place we don't want to go.

Loving others is a mental and spiritual stopping point to make sure our next actions correspond to that love we are to profess. It is not an emotion but a willing act to honor someone else above ourselves.

A Prayer

Heavenly Father,

Thank You so much for giving us the commandment to love. I want to love others well to honor You and to edify the body of Christ. Lord, sometimes it is so difficult, and I feel ill-equipped to love the way I should. Please help me give myself grace, and help me to lean on You for wisdom. You asked me to love, so You will help me love when it seems impossible. Thank You.

In Jesus's name,

Amen.

DAY 4

Friends

You are My friends if you do whatever I command you.

—JOHN 15:14

JESUS IS KING. JESUS IS SAVIOR. AND JESUS IS ALSO FRIEND. HE doesn't want to have a standoffish relationship with us. His goal is to make us friends. When we follow Him, we're showing Jesus that we value Him. That we care what He's taught us, what He's made known to us, and that we believe Him.

What are the qualities you desire in a friend?

When I was younger, I desperately wanted a good friend. I moved around a lot, so making friends was *not* easy for me. I was introverted and shy (with a touch of social anxiety but didn't know that then). I had to wait for others to invite me into their friend circle.

But then I discovered how amazing God was. Jesus let me talk to Him about anything. And though I prayed for a Jonathan and David-type friendship, I slowly started to see that Jesus was my very best friend.

- I could talk to Him about anything, and He'd listen and offer the very best advice.
- I could trust Him and knew I could count on Him.
- He remained by my side during tough times and let me let all my feelings out.
- He never judged or condemned me.

There are many more reasons I can give as to why Jesus has become the dearest Friend to me, but they are my reasons. Let's talk about yours.

How has Jesus become a Friend to you? How can you deepen that relationship even more?

We cannot go through this life alone, but thanks to the Holy Spirit, we won't. Jesus calls us *friend*, but as He prepares a place for us in Heaven, He's left us with the gift of the Holy Spirit. Even in His absence, He is still looking out for our best interests. But that knowledge does not stop with us. We're to share with others about the most amazing Friend we've ever had. And the great thing about Jesus is that He doesn't have a limit on how many friends He can have.

Abiding in Jesus is a way for us to soak up every lesson, every character trait He has to offer, and incorporate it into our own selves so that when we produce fruit, that exemplifies someone who has been abiding with the Lord. This will then improve every aspect in our life, and our friendships bear that benefit as well.

How does being friends with Jesus improve our earthly friendships?

____

____

____

____

Consider this:

Call/text a friend and tell them why they mean so much to you. Thank them for going above and beyond, or simply thank them for being in your life. If you have more than one friend you wish to call, please take that step to contact them all.

Lastly, pray over any broken friendships you may have. It may be that God wishes to heal any open wounds or reconcile those relationships. Let Him guide you in that endeavor.

DAY 5

Chosen

> You did not choose Me, but I chose you and appointed you that you should go and bear fruit, and that your fruit should remain, that whatever you ask the Father in My name He may give you.
>
> —JOHN 15:16

REMEMBER IN THE FIRST WEEK HOW WE TALKED ABOUT THE TASKS the Vinedresser has? The Vinedresser, the Creator of the universe, chose you. He knew this world needed you. He knew He wanted a relationship with you. He knew that you would bear fruit. He knew you would answer the call.

> For You formed my inward parts;
> You covered me in my mother's womb.
>
> —PSALM 139:13

When I was growing up, participating in sports for PE class was the bane of my existence. If I could have somehow faded into the shadows and gone unnoticed, I would have. Yet the time would always come when the teacher saw through my evasion tactics and brought me front and center. If that wasn't bad enough, the teachers would task two people to pick teams. Oh, the turmoil! I *knew* I wasn't good at sports. Getting picked first wasn't a question. Getting picked last didn't matter either. Because no matter where I fell in the lineup, I knew I would fail my team. I'm a pure spectator and was given no physical talent at all—unless you count clumsiness as a physical talent.

Yet the God of the universe chose Me. He knew I would bear fruit and that my fruit would remain. Through the ups and downs I have faced and will face in the future, through the change in motherhood seasons, through whatever life throws my way, God knows my fruit will remain. What a blessing that is! What a relief to know that I can*not* mess this up.

Read Ephesians 2:1-10.

Grace covers us on a daily basis. There is no need for us to strive. Good works do not earn us salvation or favor with God. In fact, we were made for the task set before us. God knew we could handle what He'd planned before we were ever born.

Erase those lies the enemy keeps whispering to you. You are enough because God said so. You can do all things through Jesus Christ, because He is our strength (Philippians 4:13).

You. Have. Been. Chosen. Let that sink in to the deepest parts of your heart that are cracked and wounded. For every time you didn't feel good enough, for every time you felt lacking, for every time you felt your failures would prevent good things from happening, repeat to yourself, "I have been chosen."

What does it mean to you to be chosen?

Let God's Word redefine you. Let His truth establish your identity. Let the True Vine fill you with living water (John 7) and water all the parched places of your soul.

You can abide in God because He's got you. You can abide in Him without worry because He chose you. You can dwell with the Father, Son, and Holy Spirit because you have borne fruit and it *will* remain.

> Being confident of this very thing, that He who has begun a good work in you will complete it until the day of Jesus Christ.
>
> — PHILIPPIANS 1:6

My Prayer for You

Heavenly Father,

I pray this study has enriched the person reading this right now. I pray their spiritual life has grown and will continue to grow. I pray this study acts as a stepping stone to a deeper relationship with You: the Father, the Son, and the Holy Spirit. I pray they will return to these pages when they need a reminder of where they belong and how they fit in the vineyard. May they always remember they were chosen for this.

In Jesus's name, I pray,

Amen.

BIBLIOGRAPHY

Gilby, Caroline. "Winemaking: The Importance of the Soil," *The Wine Society*, June 22, 2020. https://www.thewinesociety.com/discover/explore/expertise/winemaking-the-importance-of-the-soil.

"A Hebrew and English Lexicon of the Old Testament," entry for "yacaph," accessed June 17, 2024, Bible Study Tools, https://www.biblestudytools.com/lexicons/hebrew/kjv/yacaph.html.

"A Hebrew and English Lexicon of the Old Testament," entry for "yare," Bible Study Tools, Salem Media Group, accessed June 15, 2024, https://www.biblestudytools.com/lexicons/hebrew/kjv/yare.html.

Helwi, Pierre. "Cover Crops for Vineyard Floor Management," College of Agriculture & Life Sciences, Texas A&M University, October 2017, https://aggie-horticulture.tamu.edu/vitwine/2018/09/17/cover-crops-for-vineyard-floor-management/.

Merriam-Webster.com Dictionary, entry for "branch," accessed May 10, 2024, https://www.merriam-webster.com/dictionary/branch.

Merriam-Webster.com Thesaurus, entry for "pests," accessed May 5, 2024, https://www.merriam-webster.com/thesaurus/pests.

Merriam-Webster.com Dictionary, entry for "prune," accessed May 11, 2024, https://www.merriam-webster.com/dictionary/prune.

Merriam-Webster.com Thesaurus, entry for "scion," accessed May 5, 2024, https://www.merriam-webster.com/thesaurus/scion.

Merriam-Webster.com Thesaurus, entry for "set apart," accessed April 2, 2024, https://www.merriam-webster.com/thesaurus/set%20apart.

Merriam-Webster.com Dictionary, entry for "vinedresser," accessed July 24, 2024, https://www.merriam-webster.com/dictionary/vinedresser.

New Testament Greek Lexicon – King James Version," entry for "auxano," Bible Study Tools, Salem Media Group, accessed June 15, 2024, https://www.biblestudytools.com/lexicons/greek/kjv/auxano.html.

"The Older the Vine, the Better the Wine...Truth or Fiction?," Last Bottle, posted February 4, 2016, https://blog.lastbottlewines.com/education/old-vines-better-wine/.

Orr, James, ed., *International Standard Bible Encyclopedia*, entry for "abide", Bible Study Tools, Salem Media Group, 10 June 2024, https://www.biblestudytools.com/dictionary/abide/.

"Pruning and Canopy Management," Western Agriculture Research Center, Montana State University, accessed June 15, 2024. https://agresearch.montana.edu/warc/guides/grapes/managing-vineyard/canopy-management.html.

"Talking Terroir: The Dirt on Soil for Wine," King Estate Winery, posted November 29, 2016, https://kingestate.com/talking-terroir-the-dirt-on-soil/.

Webster's Unabridged Dictionary (Project Gutenberg, 2009), entry for "patience," last updated June 28, 2023, https://www.gutenberg.org/cache/epub/29765/pg29765-images.html#chap16.

"What is called the aspect of a vineyard?," Oray-Wine, posted August 19, 2023. https://oray-wine.com/en/what-is-called-the-aspect-of-a-vineyard/.

ACKNOWLEDGMENTS

I would love to thank the small-group leaders in the women's ministry at Holy Trinity Church for encouraging me to write this study. As someone who loves fiction and has written over thirty fictional books, entering the world of nonfiction was daunting. But the prayers, the encouragement, and the absolute faith you've shown in me has kept me going. This is for you!

Thank you to Carrie Schmidt for taking the time to read this study. I so value your insights and encouragement, dear friend. I'm so blessed to know you.

Thank you also to Brianna Goodwin and Sarah Keimig for your insights as well! Blessings to you both.

To my husband and boys, thank you for giving me the time to write. I love you to the moon and back!

ABOUT THE AUTHOR

Toni Shiloh is a wife, mom, and an award-winning Christian contemporary romance author. Her novel *In Search of a Prince* won the first ever Christy Amplify award. It has been praised by Oprah Daily, POPSUGAR, Library Journal, and Booklist, and is a Parable Group bestseller. Her books have been finalists for the Holt Medallion and the Selah Award. As a member of American Christian Fiction Writers (ACFW) and Faith, Hope & Love Christian Writers (FHLCW), Toni loves connecting with readers and authors alike via social media. Learn more at http://tonishiloh.com.

ALSO BY TONI SHILOH

Christy Award-winning novels

In Search of a Prince

To Win a Prince

Full list of books at

http://tonishiloh.com/books